Pelican Books
Freedom in a Rocking Boat

Sir Geoffrey Vickers was born in 1894 and educated at Oundle School and Merton College, Oxford. During the First World War he served with the Sherwood Foresters and other regiments, and in 1915 he won the V.C.

After the war he became a solicitor and spent the next twenty years of his professional life mainly as a partner in a large firm of corporation lawyers in the City of London. In the Second World War he was re-commissioned and embarked on a new career in administration, as Head of Economic Intelligence at the Ministry of Economic Warfare and as a member of the Joint Intelligence Committee of the Chiefs of Staff. In 1945 he was knighted. He then joined the National Coal Board, first as legal adviser and later as the member responsible for manpower, training, education, health and welfare.

Since his retirement in 1955 Sir Geoffrey has combined his writing and lecturing activities with part-time directorships. He has been a member of many public and professional bodies, including the Medical Research Council, the London Passenger Transport Board, and the Councils of the Law Society and the Royal Institute of International Affairs. He has been much concerned with social aspects of medicine, psychiatry and mental health, and from 1952 to 1967 he was Chairman of the Research Committee of the Mental Health Research Fund.

Sir Geoffrey is a frequent contributor to learned journals and is the author of the following books: *The Undirected Society* (1959), *The Art of Judgement* (1965), *Towards a Sociology of Management* (1967) and *Value Systems and Social Process* (1968).

Freedom in a Rocking Boat

Geoffrey Vickers

Changing Values in an Unstable Society

Penguin Books

Penguin Books Ltd, Harmondsworth,
Middlesex, England
Penguin Books Inc., 7110 Ambassador Road,
Baltimore, Maryland 21207, U.S.A.
Penguin Books Australia Ltd, Ringwood,
Victoria, Australia

First published by Allen Lane The Penguin Press 1970
Published in Pelican Books 1972

Made and printed in Great Britain by
Hazell Watson & Viney Ltd,
Aylesbury, Bucks
Set in Monotype Imprint

FOR MY DAUGHTER PAMELA,

to whom I am more happily indebted
than I could tell or she would credit

Contents

'That which lies before the human race is a constant struggle to maintain and improve, in opposition to the state of Nature, the state of Art of an organised polity.'

T. H. Huxley, 1893
Prolegomena to Ethics and Evolution

A note on form

As a reader, I dislike footnotes. If in mid-page I shift my attention to the foot of the page, I seldom find the result worth the interruption. If I do not, I wonder but never know what I have missed. To spare the reader similar distress, I have transferred to the end of each chapter, where it can most easily be read, skimmed or skipped, any material which belongs to the chapter but which, for the sake of clarity, has been kept out of the text; and I am content that the reader should leave it there, until he comes to it.

The only material which seems to need a different treatment is a note on the concept of stability, which plays a large part in the book. I have thought it best to let my understanding of this, and of the related concept of system, appear first from my use of them in successive chapters, and to add a more comprehensive summary at the end. This appears as an appendix on 'The Oddity of Historical Systems'.

Introduction

I was born in Victorian England. I have travelled in a Europe where frontiers still asked no passports and the golden sovereign was an international currency. Freedom and order, security and stability, progress and unity seemed to my young eyes to be operative standards, enjoyable realities, even natural assumptions. The illusion was total but I am glad to have known it. It has kept me fruitfully surprised by every new assertion of reality as it emerged.

The world I live in now differs from my childhood world as night from day. This difference blends most subtly gain with loss, as all who appreciate the night will know. As wartime blackout let the stars be seen again above the darkened streets, so the eclipse of our small certainties has revealed processes on an ampler scale of space and time. They are the processes of regulation on which order depends – not this order or that but any order which humans may aspire to impose on life, at any level from the planetary to the personal, in any aspect from the economic to the ethical. It is with these regulative processes that this book is concerned. I think I understand them better for seeing them against the background of that dazzling false dawn.

It is high time to explore them, for they are manifestly breaking down – so much so that I cannot guess, as I write these words in April 1968, the levels or the aspects at which new disorder will have erupted before the book is published or even finished. Moreover we have today new ways of understanding these regulative processes which we urgently need to use and to spread.

This is a personal book, though perhaps not more so than

most books. A writer may try his best to draw a map of how things are, that will be equally valid for all; but all he can really do is to paint a picture of what he sees from the unique and transient viewpoint which is his alone. Being human is equally a personal experience. It is for the reader to say how much my view contributes to his own. Yet the only reason why I write the book or why anyone should read it is that, however partial and personal, it reviews a predicament which, as I believe, involves all humans alive today as no common fate has ever done before. To be human *now*, in the last third of the twentieth century, is to share a common threat – not primarily the threat of nuclear war – and a common responsibility so great as to transcend the imperatives of our warring political ideologies and our obsolescent economic mythologies, and to need with corresponding urgency a common understanding of them. To this understanding I would make such contribution as I can.

An introduction is the place for acknowledgements; but my sense of indebtedness leaves me dumb. Socialized and humanized by being claimed from birth onwards as a member of so many communicating human groups; ushered into self-awareness through a language, every word of which resonates with the meanings of ancient usage; heir to several cultural traditions, each far too abundant for my assimilation – how can I name or number or know the living and the dead who have shaped my thoughts and me?

One debt at least I can identify and am glad to acknowledge. It is due, with many other less explicit, to Professor Adolph Lowe, whose enduring faith in freedom as a positive, ordering process crystallized and ultimately qualified the still somewhat different view expressed in the last chapter of this book.

Goring-on-Thames October 1969
England

Part I The Trap

Lobster pots are designed to catch lobsters. A man entering a man-sized lobster pot would become suspicious of the narrowing tunnel, he would shrink from the drop at the end; and if he fell in, he would recognize the entrance as a possible exit and climb out again – even if he were the shape of a lobster.

A trap is a trap only for creatures which cannot solve the problems that it sets. Man-traps are dangerous only in relation to the limitations on what men can see and value and do. The nature of the trap is a function of the nature of the trapped. To describe either is to imply the other.

I start with the trap, because it is more consciously familiar; we the trapped tend to take our own state of mind for granted – which is partly why we are trapped. With the shape of the trap in our minds, we shall be better able to see the relevance of our limitations and to question those assumptions about ourselves which are most inept to the activity and the experience of being human now.

1 The Hope that Failed

'Nobody who has paid any attention to the peculiar features of our present era will doubt for a moment that we are living in a period of most wonderful transition, which tends rapidly to accomplish that great goal to which all history points – the realization of the unity of mankind.' There has been, I believe, only one place and time in the history of men on earth when this generous and altruistic hope could have been thus confidently expressed, not by a wild prophet but by an orthodox political figure, and applauded by the representatives of a national Establishment.

The date was 1851; the speaker was the Prince Consort; the occasion was the opening of the Great Exhibition. The hope lay not in the expansion of any political power but in the peaceful interdependence of men, through the freedom of complementary trade. Behind this belief lay the faith in other allied freedoms, of opinion, of speech and of inquiry, all of which seemed to be equally benign and equally potent to support a growing but self-regulating 'order'.

The radiant vision was never so widely shared as the words suggest. On the contrary, a chorus of protest had been swelling already for a hundred years and has been growing ever louder in the troubled century since they were spoken.[1] This book is one more tributary to that turbulent stream. Undoubtedly also the vision, like all such visions, was contaminated by smugness, hypocrisy and rationalized self-interest. None the less, it rested on a reasoned and widely held interpretation of contemporary trends; it was held by acute and powerful minds; and it forms a convenient starting-point for an exploration of our present haunted but disenchanted state. For the basic misunderstandings which underlay that rosy view are easier to see in retrospect than in the contemporary scene, but they are with us still.

Today far more than a century ago, 'no one . . . will doubt for a moment that we are living in a period of most wonderful transition'. Equally, no one will doubt for a moment that the outstanding effect of this transition has been to multiply the number, variety and novelty of the interactions between individuals, groups, nations and races and their mutual interdependence. But this increase in relatedness shows at present no sign of realizing 'the unity of mankind'. On the contrary, it is marked as never before by the deepening of division and the sharpening of conflict between nations, races, groups and generations. These conflicts become increasingly revolutionary and ideological, marked by breakdown of communication at any level above that at which words are used as weapons. Even international trade, once hailed as the solvent of political strife and the mediator of economic cooperation, takes its place in the comprehensive pattern of compulsive conflict.

Thus the developments which many good minds foresaw a century ago have moved faster than they dreamed but with results the reverse of all they hoped.

The reasons for this can be stated now with some assurance.

The mid-Victorians were right in sensing that they lived at a turning point in human history. In their age men had transcended the most obvious limitation of human power. The physical energy available to them, so long substantially limited by human and animal muscle power, could now be multiplied without any obvious limit; and with this would come the indefinite increase of everything which energy could do. They realized also, though less clearly, that they had devised a new system for putting that energy to work in the multiplication of material wealth. They realized further that this would involve progressive, accelerating and partly unpredictable change. But the threat latent in this escalation of the rate of change was largely hidden from them. They did not ask what are the limitations on what energy can do. They did not understand even as well as we do today the kind of regulation needed to preserve the coherence of any system, and particularly of a system in rapid change. They understood still less the special requirements of social systems, dependent as they are on human communication and on the shared systems of interpretation which give communication meaning. In so far as they did appreciate these things, the knowledge was muted by their mistaken belief that they had solved the problem of peaceful change both economically and politically. In any case, they were already in the power of the system they had created.

A century later we can see well enough the trap which they were preparing for their successors. We have the experience and the conceptual tools to interpret it. The changes they initiated were to create a world which is neither stable nor regulable at any level or in any aspect. Each organized population, whatever its form of government, faces increasing problems of internal regulation, and these are compounded by their inability to regulate external relations which they could formerly ignore but which are now essential to their existence. Some of these problems are ecological; they arise from the relations of growing populations to their increasingly crowded and polluted living space. Some are political, concerned with the regulation of public power both internally, where the need for regulation makes it increasingly dominant, and externally, where it increasingly conflicts with others. Yet other of these problems are economic; for the economic system proves to be ever less 'automatically' regulable, either internally or externally, and in both fields the machinery for deliberate regulation is unequal to the demands on it. The most fundamental of all regulative problems are social and personal. These are the problems of setting standards, sufficiently self-consistent, attainable, valid and widely acceptable, to preserve the coherence through time and change of men and their societies. These in turn are part of those shared systems of interpreting experience on which all cooperative action and all effective communication depend. Such systems remain coherent through changing circumstances only among closely knit and mutually accepting groups; hence the passionate demand for cultural autonomy by ever smaller ethnic and other societies, and its ever sharper clash with the demand of the economic system for ever larger and more standardized populations of consumers. Each set of regulative problems excites the others and all are heightened by their combined effect on the integrity of individuals. This complex of instabilities is the predicament involved in being human now.

The trap in its basic nature is the same in every case. Whether we focus attention on the individual or on any larger human association up to the whole population of the planet, we find that its relations with its environment are changing and that these changes threaten it in three main ways. Sometimes they threaten the physical basis of its existence, such as food supply, living space or even breathable air. Often they threaten the institutional basis for its existence, by posing tasks which its institutions, political, economic or social, cannot be adapted to do. Always they threaten what I will call the appreciative basis for its existence (the word 'cultural' would be too narrow) by requiring it to revise and revalue, more radically than time permits, its understanding of the world it lives in and of whatever in that world it lives for.

The main source of these destabilizing changes was the wealth-producing system, which developed, first in Britain, with such marked acceleration from the early nineteenth century. It had three main elements: private capitalism, the market economy and technological innovation. Though none of these was new, each was raised to a new power and each thus became more potent to excite the others.

Private capitalism was transformed by a revolutionary legal invention, the effect of which is even yet not fully appreciated. Until the middle of the nineteenth century, the right to form corporations and especially profit-making corporations with limited liability had been a jealously guarded privilege, extended in individual cases only by Royal Charter or special Act of Parliament. From then onwards any group of citizens could bring into being for any lawful purpose a new legal entity, capable of growing and of accumulating wealth on a scale unlimited either in size or in time. The legal status of these organizations concealed their true status as autonomous political and social entities, a new class of citizen destined to overshadow and control their creators.

The market was transformed by technological changes which made the world for a time one market place, in which the complementary character of international trade stressed its cooperative, rather than its competitive aspect. Technology itself was to be transformed by an increasing association with science, from which it had previously been dissociated to an uncanny degree.[2] And this was to create a new and mutually exciting relation between technology and science, which was to speed the growth and modify the direction of both.

These were the main constituents of the system which was to make available to mankind the products of expanding mechanical power and technological expertise. It is today by far the most powerful and characteristic feature of our age, though perhaps also the most vulnerable. Its constituents are not individuals but corporations. These corporations own much of the wealth of the world. The largest of them are more wealthy than most nation states. They are not tools but agents, making their own terms not only with customers but with governments and employees, including those in their own highest seats of power, whose roles they largely prescribe. On their continued growth governments depend for their revenues, no less than the citizens for their livings.

The System they compose spews from one spout a huge abundance of natural and unnatural products and sprays from another spout the tokens with which to buy them. It has displaced, though not replaced, the natural world as the immediate environment of Western man. It has involved each individual in a system of proliferating, faceless power, exercised increasingly not through the agencies of government but through the uncontrolled working of the System itself. For good and ill, this system is the primary source, directly and indirectly, of the accelerating changes which are overwhelming the regulative powers of political and social institutions.

Men of the nineteenth century were not unaware of the threats inherent in the powers they were releasing; but they were upheld by several hopes, all closely related and all doomed to disappointment.

They believed that the market economy would be self-regulating, as well as self-exciting; that it would discourage the production of what was not wanted, as well as encouraging the output of what was wanted. They exaggerated the extent to which market valuations reflected all the values involved in a market transaction. They ignored the extent to which its mechanisms could neither express the demand nor induce the supply of the ever-growing class of 'goods' which can only be collectively demanded or provided.

With even less justification, they believed that a political system – any political system – could equally be made self-regulating, by copying the institutions of parliamentary democracy. They believed that growing science, by adding to the corpus of human knowledge, would provide mankind with an ever broader basis for common action, and would eliminate 'irrational' thought and behaviour, even if it did not directly add to the sum of human wisdom. They exaggerated the power of these regulators and ignored or underrated the role of social regulators in making societies function and mediating the transfer of knowledge, skill and ethic from one generation to another. All these errors had one feature in common, a radically defective idea of the individual – or rather, a set of ideas which, however inconsistent with each other, had one defect in common.

The economic man is the most familiar and explicit of the Victorian models.[3] He was supposed to know what he wanted and to know what disposal of his resources would best satisfy his wants. He had no economic wants which could not be satisfied through the market. All he needed was access to a market of goods and services which, being 'free', would be responsive to his wants and to a labour market which, being also 'free', would be responsive to what he had to offer. In a later chapter I contrast this with today's realities (Ch. 12). I refer to it here only to stress that the economic man was an 'atomic' concept, a separate entity, related to his fellows only through the working of the market. His wants were his own affair; they could *and should* be taken for granted. No one should tell him what was good for him or what he ought to want. He was and should be free to choose for himself. The market guaranteed him personal economic freedom – or so much personal freedom as it showed him to deserve by its equally impersonal assessment of his economic value to his fellows.

The political man was an animal of the same kind. He too was supposed to know what he wanted. He needed only a vote and a secret ballot to give his wants as much weight as any one man's wants should have. Once again, his prime need was conceived as freedom from coercion by other men, by society or by tradition. His political, like his economic, wants were his own affair. No one should tell him what was good for him or what he ought to want; though where collective choices were involved, a majority of his fellows could properly tell him what he must put up with.

The religious man – indistinguishable in this respect from his cousin, the humanist – was controlled not by wants but by duties; but these also could be taken for granted. He knew what his duty was; even in difficult dilemmas, he had the means to decide 'according to his conscience' and the power to act on his own decision. His moral responsibility was itself a function of his assumed independence. He was free to follow his conscience – though this would soon lose its credibility, if it led him far from the path which the consciences of his fellows dictated.

Even the scientific man had one significant characteristic in common with these other models. He was supposed to increase the sum of knowledge by observing the world around him with eyes unstructured by authority. The fact that he learned, taught, persuaded and was persuaded, knew orthodoxy and heresy and their perils as no one had known them since the days before faith in science replaced faith in God – these things were conveniently forgotten, as they commonly still are.

All these models of man have one element in common. They imply a view both atomic and un-historical. It regards individuals as both separate and given. It views their relationships with other men as potential threats to their independence, rather than as sources of their humanity. It ignores the fact that they all begin as babies. It takes no account of the historical process which sets and changes the standards of aspiration and performance regulating their individual and collective lives in any field, economic, political, ethical or aesthetic.

Such a view could only have been held in a particular combination of circumstances. This was present only for a brief span among a small though influential section of the earth's inhabitants. It has long since passed away but its heritage still haunts us and we need to identify its chief features.

It was a time of relatively high consensus on values among the holders of political and economic power. The ballot box, like the market, is a device for optimizing solutions of conflict, where accord is assumed to be possible. Radical conflicts cannot be so resolved. When power is the only path to wealth or survival or to any value overriding the value of the consensus itself, it will not abide the processes of democracy, just as an auction sale will not suffice to distribute inadequate places in the lifeboats of a sinking ship. The view did indeed make a notable, perhaps a permanent contribution to the age-old problem of making power responsible and transmitting it peaceably; but its brief, local success masked the conditions on which it depended. Such individual autonomy in matters of value can be combined with social coherence only in societies in which consensus on values remains consistently high. This was once no rarity; it is the common condition of traditional societies. But it was precisely the condition which the System itself was set to undermine.

Further, it was an age of undeveloped land and unused resources. Human activities could develop exponentially for decades before they encountered restrictions bred by themselves; and by the time they did so, they had developed an ideology strong enough to keep the truth at bay for several more decades. Once growth as such becomes a value, every development can be seen either as growth or as the necessary price of growth. The difference between cancerous growth and ordered growth is detectable at an early stage in human bodies, because the order which is violated is biologically prescribed. In the various orders which men impose on or recognize in human life, economic, political, ethical or aesthetic, this distinction between the orderly and the proliferating is less apparent; but it is not less real.

Finally, it was an age itself defined by a unique and complex heritage. One element in this was the Judaeo-Christian tradition, with its emphasis on personal responsibility, itself hugely heightened by the manifold strands of ecclesiastical protest which were woven into the Reformation. Another element was the rise of the physical sciences and with it both an expansion of confidence in human reason and a tacit reduction in the concept of what human reason is. No Western European today can so restructure his mind as to see the world or himself or his fellows as they would appear if he had not been born into a culture which, two centuries ago, self-consciously delighted in experiencing an Age of Enlightenment. Yet in fact most of the world was untouched by that event and its assumptions are being daily eroded.

Few peoples are so handicapped in controlling their future as those once 'enlightened' Western peoples who must now reconstruct their scale of values and redirect the focus of their attention.

We have, happily, some new conceptual tools.

Newton's world consisted of bodies which remained at rest until something moved them, or in constant motion unless something changed their course. Change, not stability, needed explanation; and the explanation was given in terms of 'forces'. Our world, by contrast, consists of events which would not remain sufficiently regular even to earn a name, unless their constituents were so related as to regulate themselves. In such a world stability, or at least regularity, not change and motion demands explanation; and the explanation is given, especially in psychological and social systems, in terms of 'information' and of the interpretative systems which give information meaning.

This changed world demands new concepts with which to comprehend its features and new language with which to describe them; and these are coming into use from the study of systems of many kinds, biological, psychological, economic, political, social – and even technological. For the human mind is hard put to it to think of anything which it cannot model.

The systems of communication and control embodied in space satellites and weapon systems and automatic factories make their contribution to the models we use for thinking about systems of much greater importance. It is probably their most important use, both for good and for ill.

For the study of communication makes it clear that any communication depends on the system of interpretation which gives it meaning; that a communication, as distinct from a transmission system, can only be designed by a would-be communicator who knows or thinks he knows the system of interpretation which awaits his communication at the receiving end. It must thus ultimately focus attention on systems of interpretation, their origin, growth and change. Equally, the study of control makes it clear that any control depends on the standards with which incoming information is compared. (Even the information supplied by a compass to an automatic pilot would have a different 'meaning' if supplied to a device designed to compute dead reckoning.) The peculiarity of human and social systems lies not so much in their ability to store and handle information as in their ability to evolve and change the manifold and competing standards by which they live and in the uncertainties involved in the resolution of these conflicts. And this is the prime source of their instability. We may hope then that the current study of communication and control, remote though it often is from problems of human government, may make its contribution not only by providing concepts general enough to cover all kinds of regulation but also by focusing attention on those problems of value which have so long been ignored or taken for granted. For the idea of deliberate regulation depends on and implies values, standards, criteria, whether in a Cabinet, a board room, or an industrial research and development laboratory.

A society's 'values', that linked set of criteria for determining success in any field, is itself a system, capable of orderly change but also susceptible to breakdown, needing to be understood and cared for even more carefully than the economic and political systems which depend on it. The ignored assumptions of a century ago are and should be the focus of attention today.

The overriding problem for today is how to make, from the unstable, warring systems in which we live, a governable world of governable men – at whatever level may prove possible. This will involve choice not only of the criteria for regulation but also of the areas which it is worth trying deliberately to regulate and of the costs, often equally unacceptable, of attempting to regulate them or leaving them to find their own equilibrium. These choices are not only hard and unpalatable; they are also still too often rejected as unnecessary. This book aims not so much to supply the answers as to make acceptable the fact that answers are needed and to make familiar the terms in which they must be given, the fields in which they must be sought, and the costs that must be paid.

Studies in human ecology usually begin by identifying some threatening imbalance between a population and its habitat, such as the threat of famine in India, of air pollution in Los Angeles or of water pollution in the Great Lakes. They proceed to explore the technological possibilities of dealing with the threat – the scale of effort needed, the length of time required. It is the established problem-solving technique of Western culture. But it is not the method of this book. For I believe that no degree of technological innovation and no scale of technological effort can rescue the West from its self-set trap. The solutions can only be through political, institutional and cultural change, deeply penetrating the minds of individual men and women and gaining ascendancy as quickly as is consistent with the mysterious process by which the meaning of human experience is transmuted as it passes from one generation to the next. And if this is so of threats from changes in the physical environment, it is far more true of those more numerous and sinister threats from changes in the social environment, which become increasingly dominant. We have to ask not only what these threats are and what they will do to people but also what they will mean to people – and to which people. We have to ask not only what the threatened will want to do about them but also what, given their institutions and their culture, they will be able to do about them and how quickly and in what directions their institutions and their values can be expected to change.

This inner world, in which men inescapably live, develops in intimate relationship with the physical world, yet according to its own laws and its own time scale. Human history can be understood only as the interaction of the two worlds. The inner world has its own realities, its own dynamism – and its own ecology. Like the life forms of the physical world, the dreams of men spread and colonise their inner world, clash, excite, modify and destroy each other, or preserve their stability by making strange accommodations with their rivals.[4]

The architecture of this inner world needs a more sensitive and respectful technology even than our relations with the physical earth which we have so crudely and blindly violated. But it is not beyond our influence or our duty. Its instrument is that dialogue to which this book is meant to contribute.

NOTES AND REFERENCES

1. The most recent, most eloquent and most trenchant contribution known to me is Carl Oglesby's description of the Young Rebels in W. R. Ewald (Ed.) *Environment and Change*, Indiana University Press, 1968.
2. The singular independence of technology from science until recent years is traced in S. Toulmin and J. Goodfield, *The Architecture of Matter*, Hutchinson, 1952; Pelican, 1965.
3. Economists may insist that the economic man was never intended to be a model, merely a convenient abstraction. Since no model can be more than a convenient abstraction, I do not find the distinction persuasive. Even if logically valid, it is not one which can be preserved in practice. See also p. 105.
4. Vickers, G., *Value Systems and Social Process*, Tavistock Publications, 1968, and New York, Basic Books, 1968, p. 32.

2 The Fouled Nest

I identified three fields in which accelerating rates of change threaten the bases of our continuity – the physical, the institutional and the cultural. When we try to distinguish these, we find how closely interlocked they are.

Populations of other species, developing in a favourable and unfilled habitat, tend to multiply at a constant rate until they encounter limitations of some kind. These limitations progressively restrict their rate of growth; so the general pattern of their growth curves takes the form of the letter S. But whereas the accelerating growth of the first half is common to most of such systems, the pattern of the second half varies widely. Sometimes the rate of growth flattens quickly or slowly and becomes constant. Sometimes it oscillates. Sometimes it plunges; a population which has multiplied for many generations may crash and disappear, either because in its period of growth it has developed habits which unfit it for living in a restricted environment or because its way of living has made its environment unfit to support even a limited population.

The restraining limitation may be simply the size of the territory; for example, when a bird population is restricted by the number of possible nesting sites. It may be the action of predators attracted by the increasing numbers of prey; in which case prey and predators may come to form a stable system, each controlling the size of the other. It may result from the activities of the population itself, as when a wood becomes so thick as to throw a lethal shade on its own seed bed. All these situations have rough but striking parallels in the human scene.

When fluctuations in non-human populations are closely

examined, more subtle regulators often appear. The snowshoe hares of the Arctic tundra and the lynxes which prey on them maintain a rhythmic oscillation in their numbers which engaged the attention of the Hudson's Bay Company, intent on the fur trade, long before it becomes an object of study for ecologists. It now appears that in addition to the mutual influence of prey and predator, and apparently more important, the hare population is periodically checked by biochemical changes produced somehow by increasing numbers which restrict fertility. A more dramatic example is provided by the lemmings whose periodical, suicidal rush to the sea now seems to be prompted by physiological stress provoked by their own numbers. Each lemming simultaneously finds it physically unbearable to live among so many lemmings.

The annual rush of Britons to the sea has not yet become so costly in human life as to operate as a control of population – and it never will. Long before physiological stress began to operate on such a scale, psychological and social stress would have moved us to limit our numbers in other ways; and the most obvious of these is to fight for living space, as we are already beginning to do. Studies of other species, useful as they are, do not take us far in understanding the behaviour of 'developed' human societies. The differences are fundamental. The ecological trap which our species has set itself is unique to us and we have unique, though not necessarily suitable or adequate, powers of appreciating and responding to it.

Consider first the peculiarities of the trap.

First, humans are still increasing at an accelerating rate; their doubling time is still growing shorter. It took nearly 1700 years from the beginning of the Christian era for the world's population to double from about 250 million to 500 million. The next double took only 200 years; the next 75 years, bringing the figure to about 2 billion in 1925. The next double, to 4 billion, has nearly been completed in less than 50 years. Such an explosion has no parallel among the non-human populations studied by ecologists.

An even more important difference, of course, is the impact which this development and its causes are having on mankind's physical home, which is the other term of the relationship. On the one hand, men have amplified its capacity to support them at a rate which has increased overall even more rapidly than the population. On the other hand, they have exploited and damaged this potential to an extent which cannot yet be assessed.

This apocalyptic mixture of promise and threat has only recently begun to disturb the complacency of the West. The first threat to be seriously noticed was the possible threat to food supplies. The next was the possible exhaustion of raw materials, especially of the fossil fuels. Each was countered by the confident promise of technology to match multiplying wants with increased food productivity, to substitute abundant materials for rare ones, synthetic for natural ones, and to multiply available energy far beyond the resources of the fossil fuels. So far these promises have been met – but only if we accept, as we should not do, a balance sheet which ignores all costs which have not yet had to be paid and all problems of distribution. The costs ignored are the accumulative, self-limiting costs of pollution. The distributive problems are those which are ignored by assuming that humanity is one system in which the production and distribution of goods to match needs is limited only by technological, rather than by political, institutional and cultural factors.

Projections of future population trends are notoriously unreliable, though hitherto the most dramatic errors have been underestimates. But if we consider not the trends but the innovations which may increase or reduce populations, those that make for increase are still dominant. These are notably the power to reduce infant mortality, to increase food supply and to prolong old age. All these free population growth from the restraints of famine and disease, restraints which are still operating in most countries where growth is a major problem. Against this the technologies of birth control seem a small factor, except in countries where families larger than the replacement rate are not encouraged by the culture or by the economic and social structure of society. Such countries are in a minority and already present little problem.

A less noticed difficulty in population control is the increasing need of developed countries for *predictable and fairly stable* populations. The more the individual relies on the collective provision of basic needs, the more essential stability becomes. Homes must match households with some precision. Everyone needs a home; very few need more than one. Equally, homes must match workplaces, at least so long as someone in most families works; schools must match homes and teachers must match schools. Fluctuations which cause local disparities in these fields cannot be made good quickly by the elasticity of market machinery; they have to be planned for far in advance. Nor can 'mis-match' be endured in these fields safely or for long. Homes and schools are not luxuries.

Thus apart from all problems of population *growth*, the fluctuation of populations sets insoluble problems to the regulators of a modern state. Yet these fluctuations would seem to depend chiefly on individual powers of discretion which will be heightened and thus made less, not more, predictable by better contraception. In a country where birth control is easy and universally practised, populations, in so far as they depend on this factor, are likely to fluctuate more, not less, than they do now – unless, of course, the increased *power* is matched by increased *control*, a prospect which is anathema to Western nations. Fluctuation poses threats, whatever the level of population, threats not to food supply but to resources equally important both to individuals and to society. The imbalance of resources is paid for in institutional and cultural damage.

There are problems still unsolved in regulating the supply, still more the distribution, of food, raw materials and power to meet the needs of an exploding or even an unpredictably fluctuating population; but the solution of these problems generates further problems which are even more serious and intractable. These are the problems of pollution. They are more serious because they are seldom soluble by technology, within the assumptions that technology sets itself. For pollution is a function of activity; and developing technology is predicated on still more activity. Noise is a form of pollution; but to abate noise by abating activity is the least obvious and the least acceptable solution for a technological society. In any case it is questionable whether there is any technological answer to the degree of pollution inseparable from the numbers and activities of men as they are today, even without allowing for any increase in either.

We may be sure that the full story of pollution is not yet known and can never be known until long after the event, when damage may be irretrievable; but the main current concerns can be briefly summarized.[1]

The pollution of space is at present largely, though not entirely, the concern of astronomers. They have also benefited from other aspects of the same activites. Few fields show better the ambivalent nature of technology's blessings when administered by the System.

In 1958 instruments carried by a space probe revealed for the first time that the earth is enclosed, at distances far outside its atmosphere, by zones consisting of belts of electrons, now known as the Van Allen belts. Not many months later the USA exploded a hydrogen bomb between the Van Allen belts and added (contrary to their scientists' confident predictions) a new belt of charged particles, thus changing in ways important to astronomers the basic situation in which they were working. The catalogue of scientific complaints against the military in both the USA and the USSR is not confined to this. It is conceivable that by the time space technology has provided automatic or even manned observations in space, its activities will have made useless all the radio telescopes on earth. If so, it will elegantly typify the kind of thing technology does when used as it now is.

To non-astronomers the chief significance of the story is to show, first, how unreliable are the predictions of scientists concerning the side-effects of technological actions, and secondly how little institutional or cultural control there is over such actions, where the result of control would be to curtail even slightly an exploding technology. The two themes are linked and recur again and again in the dreary story of pollution. Scientists are as prone as anyone else to human frailty and even to intellectual error. They owe their reputation for responsibility and for accuracy to the tradition which exposes their thought, step by step, to the criticism of their scientific colleagues. When they become the servants of political or industrial masters, pursuing limited goals under conditions of secrecy, they become a public danger.

Other activities in space have more direct human implications. The radiation hazard from atomic explosions in the atmosphere has already taken its toll of human life and made its mark on human genetics. These hazards also were first denied and acknowledged only after the event, when the independent studies of scientists outside the defence machine forced politicians and official scientists to acknowledge the error. Further pollution of this kind is consequently limited for the present (except in the event of nuclear war) to powers outside the test ban treaty.

Space exploration has another uncharted hazard. It seems that no one knows with sufficient precision how dependent our earth is, for protection against ultra-violet radiation from space, on the ozone layer, which surrounds it outside its own atmosphere, or how vulnerable this layer may be to the passage of large rockets carrying satellites. Mistakes in this area are not likely to be predictable or reparable or tolerable. American 'Fears of Soviet Gains in Moon Race' – to quote a recent headline in *The Times* – will seem misdirected if the combined efforts of the competitors make their joint home intolerable for them both and for the rest of us. Here is another field in which it seems that we may now have the power to disrupt one of the basic conditions of life on the planet but not the knowledge or the institutions or the cultural controls to prevent the power from being used blindly and irresponsibly for the sake of one country's technological prestige.

A little nearer home, we have hitherto been able to take for granted the air we breathe. This is now at risk in at least two ways. The poisons released into it, notably by internal combustion engines, create a pall over the large cities in which we are increasingly to live, which, when atmospheric conditions combine, can already produce lethal hazards. Apart from this, our technological way of living is already interfering with the process by which the world's oxygen supply is maintained. Even the most advanced technology would be hard put to it to provide us with a substitute for oxygen.

The world's supply of oxygen is regenerated largely by

plants and by the plankton in the oceans. Millions of acres of grassland and suburbanized woodland go under concrete yearly in the United States alone; and the great rain forests may be eroded sooner than we expect if the technological explosion does not breed some other reversal. At the same time the oceans and lakes are increasingly poisoned by detergents, pesticides and industrial wastes. On the other hand, the carbon oxides in the atmosphere are greatly increased by the combustion of fossil fuels.

One result of this process is that the carbon dioxide in the atmosphere slowly increases, encasing the earth in an invisible greenhouse. The average annual temperature has risen by one degree over the last fifty years, during which time the carbon dioxide has increased by ten per cent. It is not certain how closely these two events are connected. In any case, since some parts of the earth, especially the poles, would be more comfortable if they were warmer, the prospect may elicit from those of us who dwell in temperate zones only a faint and largely altruistic satisfaction, linked perhaps with a detached concern for the penguins. The detachment would be misplaced. If the carbon dioxide in the atmosphere were to double, it is thought that the polar ice would melt. The polar ice cap, melted, would raise the level of the world's oceans by 200–300 feet and drown most of humanity's past and much of its present. The change would hide much unsightliness and give us a wonderful chance to start many things again. But England would be much smaller and an unfamiliar shape, if ocean-going vessels docked at Reading, York and Darlington.[2]

Next to air and open space, we are accustomed to take for granted the salt water of the oceans. We can do so no longer. These too are being brought within our 'socio-technical system', and provide a new field for the endemic human situation, in which multiple uses conflict with each other and their resultant pollution conflicts with all. Large areas of the sea bed are being exploited for mining. The farming of the sea for food is in the middle distance in the speculations of food technologists. Meantime oil-fired then diesel-driven ships contribute to the pollution of its surface, supplemented by the inevitable periodic loss of ever larger tankers. The detergents used to protect the tourist industry from oil-fouled beaches are worse for the fish and the plankton than the oil. Perhaps radioactive waste, dumped deliberately from nuclear reactors or accidentally by the misfortunes of nuclear submarines and bombers carrying nuclear warheads on their 'defensive' missions, will ultimately prove more damaging than the oil and the detergents.

Fresh water has always been a precious, usually a scarce and often a limiting factor in human life; and it is very unequally distributed. Men's earliest technology, which Lewis Mumford has contrasted so favourably with the later technology of the machine age, consisted largely in water distribution. Developed countries can no longer concern themselves merely with water *distribution*. They must control the whole water cycle.

For many millennia the river Thames has earned its name as a continuing entity. It is in fact the way in which water from a stable catchment area finds its way to the sea. . . . Throughout this time until very recently its valley provided a habitat for many species, including men, who long ago learned to live above its floodmarks and to cultivate its alluvial soil. Then we began to incorporate this river, once an independent variable, into our own man-made socio-technical system. We controlled its floods with barrages and dykes. We adapted it for transportation. We distributed its water. We used it as a sewer. Our demands rose and began to conflict with each other, making necessary, for example, the control of pollution. Now these demands have begun to conflict in total with the volume of the river. We plan to supplement it by pumping out the deep reservoirs. Soon, unless some other solution appears, we shall be supplementing its flow by pumping desalted water from the sea. By then the Thames as an independent physical system, part of the given environment, will have virtually disappeared within a human socio-technical system, dependent on new physical constructions, new institutions and a new attitude to the use of water and the regulation of the whole water cycle.[3]

The pollution of water illustrates the peculiar challenge which pollution poses. To control the flooding of the Thames we had only to discipline the river. To control its pollution we have to discipline ourselves and notably the industrial processes which are the pride of our technology. This poses not technological but political and cultural problems. Of course, even in controlling technology, we need technology. If we are to recirculate our sewage as drinking water, the technologists must clean it for us. But the basic remedy is not technological but political and, more radically, institutional and social.

The pollution of water increases the oxygen shortage; for more than half the oxygen produced by photosynthesis is made by minute organisms in the water. The destruction of these by wastes reduces the oxygen resources of the water and the life which it can support. The pollution grows worse as more water has to be stored in reservoirs, where the pollution cannot be quickly flushed away. Even where these problems are gradual, they are not necessarily slow; for any exponential growth soon accelerates alarmingly. But sometimes critical thresholds are passed which occasion sudden changes. In that great natural reservoir, Lake Erie, the deposits of pollution at the bottom, 'a kind of huge underwater cesspool',[4] are separated from the upper layer by a natural barrier a compound of iron, which is itself dependent on the oxygen in the water. The oxygen is decreasing and the barrier, is beginning to break. When it breaks, most of the living things in the lake will die. The cesspool will no longer be under water.

Far more serious in its possibilities and more illuminating in its history is the prospective pollution of earth, water and living organisms, including man, by radiation. Britain, well endowed with fossil fuels, has taken the lead with an expanding programme of nuclear reactors, both as a source of domestic energy and as a potential export. The decision was made – or at least 'justified' – on economic grounds, by comparison with operating costs of fossil fuels; but the calculation took no account of the increase in the level of radiation which the programme must entail, apart from accidents, even within so short a period as thirty years; or of the specific hazards, although these are such that no insurance company will cover them. By the year 2000 it is envisaged that atomic power production will be generating 40,000 tons of radioactive waste per year, in 10,000 reactors each of which, after a life of at most thirty years, will itself be an abandoned radioactive heap.

This accumulating waste will remain active for centuries; there is no way to neutralize it and no way to contain it which can be expected to be immune to leakage at some time. Living creatures concentrate radioactive substances in their tissues and pass them on for further concentration in the tissues of those that eat them. No international agreement has yet been reached on how to dispose of this waste; British and American proposals are bitterly opposed by most other countries. No figure can be put on this huge future and contingent cost, so it is omitted; and the programme marches on. At the same time, our government cut by half an annual appropriation of £4 million for research into the possibility of building a fusion reactor, which, if it were successful, would produce a negligible amount of radioactive waste and could be safely dismantled at the end of its life. Again the decision was 'justified' on economic grounds; the scientists concerned would produce a satisfactory return on their cost more surely and sooner if they were employed otherwise.[5]

The surface of the land, man's home and partner for so many centuries, records most clearly the wavering fortunes in the battle between accumulation and attrition. Even through the agricultural epoch's ten millennia, the balance did not always move in favour of accumulation; some of the granaries of the Roman Empire are deserts today. But in the best cultivated parts of the older countries the legacy may have been on the whole accumulative. Today it is moving adversely, despite the agricultural revolution of the last fifty years. The crudest forms of self-defeating exploitation may have been charted now, the kinds that left dis-afforested or exhausted soil to be blown or washed away. But in the agricultural partnership with nature, on which man still depends as completely as he has done for the last ten millennia, the ecological balance is threatened by technological innovations, some of which will not show their effect for decades. The 'silent Spring'[6] tells of what it has done to our fellow creatures; we do not yet know all it is doing to us.

But we do know some of the story. We know that the massive and increasing doses of nitrogenous fertilizers, on which agriculture depends today, are not only contributing to the pollution of the water supply but are raising the nitrogen level in food to a dangerous degree. (Tinned vegetable baby foods on sale in Montreal have been condemned for containing more than the permitted maximum.) Even in Sweden, a country highly alert to such risks, the concentration in fish of mercury from agricultural pollution is already interfering with the supply of a staple article of diet. In one large lake fish were found to contain one hundred times the maximum amount of mercury permitted by the World Health Organization. Whether the use of inorganic fertilizers on anything like the present scale is good in the long-term interests of farming is a question fiercely contested by 'organic' farmers. But it is not debatable that the whole agricultural economy of the developed world, the distribution of its manpower between agriculture and industry and its agricultural output and costs – not to speak of the fortunes of a large industry – have become geared to a method of farming which generates self-defeating, deferred costs and ignores them, because they will fall into someone else's accounts.

The relation between men and the urban environment is even more unstable than that between them and the natural environment – and for the same reason. The activities which the city expresses change it and change the needs (and thus the activities) of those who live in it on a destabilizing scale. They generate traffic which the city cannot accommodate. They generate waste which the city cannot dispose of. They generate demands for conflicting land use, of which the city can satisfy an ever smaller part. They generate conflicting desires which the city cannot satisfy, and these frustrations generate disgust and desire to escape, which the city can only frustrate.[7]

In theory, the city could be so planned as to provide a far better combination of answers to these competing demands than it commonly does today; and undoubtedly it will be the major task of the immediate future to try to realize some of these possibilities. We do not lack the physical means to build and to demolish. In practice, what we can achieve depends on institutional and cultural changes which are still beyond us and which can be had even in theory at a price which few

Westerners are yet prepared to pay or even to contemplate. It involves not only the creation of radically new ways to impose form on the urban environment but also the harsh curtailment of the ways on which we have relied and in which so many interests are invested.

Until recent years the urban environment expanded chiefly by building on undeveloped land and secondarily by replacing existing buildings with new ones. Communications between buildings could be left to take care of themselves, almost as waterborne traffic could be left to find its way in coastal waters. Today the urban environment has to be planned in large areas and in four dimensions; for projected needs changing with time must be considered no less than extension upward and downward. Many uses have to be considered together, notably access to the buildings matching the activities which they generate. Yet this is only one of their many competing needs. As each sector of the urban environment becomes more dependent on the others, it becomes harder to make any significant change, except on an ever larger scale and with increasing disruption and cost in many currencies. Even the conception of the city itself, as an entity bounded and supported by the basic rural world, seems to be dissolving, giving place to the concept of urban space, extending indefinitely, within which social and political divisions may have no more natural validity than the frontiers which colonial powers left behind in Africa. For good and ill, the urban environment which will come into being, planned or unplanned, in the next thirty years is likely to determine the physical living space of Western man for many decades. For the rate at which men can remake an urban environment already made and occupied is limited by the fact that they must go on living in it in the meantime.

There is no need to multiply or elaborate further these familiar examples. They mark the inherent instability of the relations of technological man with his physical surroundings. Human activities disturb the conditions on which their own continuance depends. Moreover, the more man-made the environment, the greater its instability. It used to be hoped, even assumed, that men would have the greatest control in the area over which they could exercise the greatest power. This confusion of power and control still haunts minds which might be expected to have outgrown it. Dr Edmund Leach opened his Reith lectures in 1967 with these words:[8]

> Men have become like gods. Isn't it about time that we understood our divinity? Science offers us total mastery over our environment and our destiny, yet instead of rejoicing, we feel deeply afraid. Why should this be? How might these fears be resolved?

It sounds like the voice of the nineteenth century, scolding the twentieth for looking into the twenty-first. This is unfair to the nineteenth century. The Prince Consort was not so naïve as to confuse the power to alter with the power to control and to conceal the confusion under the word 'mastery'. His vision was of a world not 'mastered' by science but regulated by human institutions. Nor did he conceal under a royal 'we' the fact that the human race consists of political organizations which compete for a common environment and have different aspirations for their destinies and of which the most powerful have far more power over each other's destinies than over their own. The difficulty in controlling human affairs is not and has never been due to shortage of the energy needed to push things and people about. It lies in deciding what forms should be imposed on human life, among such possibilities as are open, and in generating sufficient agreement to make the chosen forms effective regulators of the action needed to impose and maintain them.

The major differences between human ecology and the ecology of other species spring from the increased rate of change which technology, as used by Western societies, has introduced into the relation of men with their physical milieu. This has set going a chain reaction of self-exciting changes in the physical world and in men's relations with it and with each other. These will soon prove self-defeating, probably through the conflicts they will engender, unless political and social regulators can establish control over the System. But our present regulators are themselves part of a system set to be self-exciting; and the impact of technology is itself a function of the system which sets it to work. In the next chapter I describe what seem to me to be the key features of this system. To Westerners they may be too familiar to question or even to notice. They are none the less unique to Western societies; they are not being widely copied elsewhere; and there is reason to think that they are obsolescent even in their homes of origin.

NOTES AND REFERENCES

1. The details which follow owe much to Professor Barry Commoner's *Science and Survival*, Gollancz, 1966. On the population explosion see also Paul B. Ehrlich, *The Population Bomb*, New York, Ballantine Books, 1968.

2. I understand that this trend now appears to have been reversed, though no one knows why. The only conclusion I wish to draw is that human activities now alter basic conditions of life in ways we neither control or understand.

3. Vickers, G., *Value Systems and Social Process*, Tavistock Publications, 1968, pp. 75, 76, and New York, Basic Books, 1968.

4. Professor Barry Commoner; lecturer at the Royal Commonwealth Society, London, 26 July 1968.

5. The issue is discussed by Dr E. F. Schumacher in the *Des Voeux Memorial Lecture*, given at the 1967 Conference of the National Society for Clean Air. See also Dr C. J. H. Watson's letter to *The Times* of 25 October 1967.

6. Rachel Carson, *The Silent Spring*, Hamish Hamilton, 1963; Penguin, 1965.

7. This fails to acknowledge the astonishing achievements of the modern city. I do so on p. 166. In many respects, modern cities are far more efficient than they were a century earlier, when they were a small fraction of their present size. None the less, the imbalances described here are real and will become increasingly intractable, as cities run short of space into which to expand. The Buchanan Report on *Traffic in Towns*, HMSO, 1963, is more than a collection of proposals for reconciling mutually conflicting activities and thus enabling more of them to be enjoyed in the same space. It is even more useful as an analysis of the multi-valued choices involved and of the ways in which they can be presented to the judgement of the policy maker.

8. *Listener*, 16 November 1967.

3 The Self-exciting System

One thing is clear from a study of systems of all kinds – no trend, literally *no* trend can be expected to continue in the same direction indefinitely, least of all one that increases at an exponential rate, however slow. So anyone who makes proposals based on the assumption that any such trend will continue should be asked to show reasonable grounds for thinking that it will at least last long enough to support whatever proposal or argument he is basing on it.

Nearly all scenarios of the future make two of these assumptions. One is that, at least in Western societies, everyone will go on getting richer and so will have more abundant personal choices. The other is that the present institutions of society will go on dealing with the society's collective choices without any change in their character so radical as to deserve attention. These forecasters do their best to startle us out of our old-fashioned assumptions about the nature of work, the scope for enjoyment, the place of authority, even the meaning of life. But they accept these linear assumptions of their own, that the system will be able to deal with the economic and the political results of its own activities.

These assumptions need to be questioned, like any other linear assumptions; first on general grounds, secondly because the trends discussed in the previous chapter and in the next suggest that they cannot be true. There is already evidence of incipient breakdown, both economic and political; and an examination of the system suggests why it should be less able to deal with the problems it is generating now than with those of the past.

It is convenient to begin by asking how it is that the System has become, in the West, so powerfully self-exciting.

The System, when stripped of its shield of familiarity, is very odd. Consider first only its two main elements. One of these is a large population of corporations which provide goods and services and recover their costs from the users, with a margin, much of which they are free to accumulate. The other element consists of institutions which also provide goods and services (including the services of government) but which recover their costs from public funds. These funds are drawn partly from the corporations which form the first element and partly from that population of individual men and women whom I have left for the moment standing in the wings of the stage, awaiting their cue to appear.

I will distinguish these two types of institution as user-supported and public-supported.[1] None of our familiar names will precisely fit. 'Public sector' and 'private sector' are the nearest approximations. Yet these are doubly misleading. Some institutions in what is commonly called the public sector, such as the railways and the Post Office, are user-supported, though others, such as the hospitals, are public-supported. In any case, it is misleading to describe as 'private' a sector consisting of autonomous corporations which perform so many public functions, and some of which are publicly controlled and even publicly owned.

The user-supported section of our economy is free to accumulate profits and increasingly finances itself out of these accumulations. These undertakings are still judged primarily by the criteria appropriate to investments; increasing turnover, profits and net wealth are accepted as their primary indices of success. So far from costing anybody anything, they are regarded as the primary producers and accumulators of wealth.

The public-supported sector is still widely regarded as living as a parasite, or perhaps a predator, on the user-supported sector. It abstracts money from the user-supported sector and uses it to provide those goods and services, including government, which the current ethos or the legacy of history regards as impossible or unsuitable to be paid for by the users. It accumulates no money, only enormous debts; and though it does accumulate vast and increasing stores of public wealth, none of these appears in any balance sheet. It is therefore not commonly regarded as either a producer or an accumulator of wealth. On the contrary, everything it does is regarded as a cost to someone.

The distinction between these two worlds was once clearer, more logical and more acceptable. Until little more than a century ago, public power performed its regulative function almost entirely by making and enforcing rules. Its control of operations was largely confined to physical coercion – law and order at home, defence (and attack) abroad. The persistence of this age-old conceptual pattern makes current developments less comprehensible and less acceptable than they would otherwise be.

The relation between these two worlds is turning into a very complex form of symbiosis. Public funds buy directly an increasing share of the user-supported products and pay the wages and salaries of an increasing proportion of all employed persons. Public authority, by redistributing the incomes of all, helps to maintain the purchasing power by which the user-supported section lives. Thus the user-supported section is increasingly dependent on the public-supported sector.

Equally, the public-supported system is increasingly dependent on the user-supported system, from which it has to get an ever-increasing annual income. It provides virtually all the common services by which the user-supported section and the general population live; roads, schools, hospitals and the rest, not to speak of defence and foreign relations. Because of the changes described in the previous chapter, the cost of maintaining all these services would rise even if both their level and the numbers served remained static. Since both numbers and aspirations rise, the public-supported services need annually not merely an increased amount but an increased proportion of the gross national product (GNP). In the West, the public-supported system extracts this at present only by taxation; and it has a far better chance of increasing its revenues from an expansion of taxable revenue than from an increase in the rates of taxation. So it has an intense, though indirect, interest in the expansion of the private sector.

The user-supported sector has a similar interest in expanding revenue and hence in expanding consumption. Competitive businesses learned long ago that they could increase their profits far more easily by expanding their total market than by winning part of a static market from a competitor. (It is rare indeed for any firm to increase its earnings in a market that is contracting or to fail to do so in a market that is expanding.) Further, the user-supported sector is dependent on growth in several other ways. Growth is necessary to capital accretion, which is also the prime attraction for investors. It is necessary to attract and keep good senior staff, who choose growing concerns because they themselves want room to grow. It is in any case the accepted yardstick of success both in the sub-culture of the user-supported sector and generally.

Again those parts of the user-supported sector which use highly capitalized mass-production processes are further dependent on growth, not only because they need long, uninterrupted runs of production but because their processes are so rigid that any output which falls short of what is planned by a quarter or even less is likely to be unprofitable. On the other hand, any demand for more than the planned output is so profitable to achieve and so damaging to refuse that it initiates intensive expansion. Thus a ratchet-like mechanism operates to make every ceiling attained into a future floor, which cannot easily be lowered. Nothing could be more conducive to self-exciting growth.

What of the men and women who individually use and pay for most of the goods and services and who, in their active capacity, fill all the seats in both sectors? Most of these also are at present motivated to increase their personal share of what is provided by the System, both to make their current lives easier and more varied and to secure themselves by accumulating their own reserves. These motivations are increased by the massive efforts of the user-supported sector, which spends £500 million a year of its consumers' money on promoting consumption. For comparison, the public-supported sector in 1968 spent £1800 million of its tax and ratepayers' money on all forms of education. This weird disparity reflects and contributes to the fact that people in Western cultures value what they buy individually so much more than what they contribute to provide collectively. The motivations of the individual are increased also by disparities of wealth no longer sanctioned by an accepted social order. They are further excited by a cultural norm which plays back to them, from other sources, the motif stated by the advertisements; and in so far as they are also agents in the user-supported sector they are influenced as consumers by the ideology which supports them as producers. To some extent they are still motivated by the search for security in an unsafe world, though for many the reaction to gathering uncertainty is to turn away from it.

Finally, affecting all sectors, is the fact that a technologically expanding world costs more to live in and more to escape from. Apart from rising expectations, increasing activity generates resistances which only more activity can overcome. The traffic jam is symbolic of a civilization self-set to overload every channel that it clears. The primitive African enjoys for nothing many 'goods which only a 'two-car family' can afford in the urban and sub-urban West, and others which are no longer attainable at any price. It does not follow that the primitive African is 'up on balance'. He is not, at least not yet. It does follow, however, that Western man in his proper effort to keep hold of simple satisfactions in his complex environment adds one other element to the self-exciting energies of the system.

There is no doubt that the System is set in a pattern of self-exciting expansion. There is equally no doubt that in the course of producing more goods and services with less effort, it has met many real needs and created or extended the range of many legitimate wants and that it has still much room to do both, even in Western countries. But we still have to ask whether the System can meet the demands which its own expansion is bringing to it, without more radical change than is consistent with the linear expectations of the prophets.

If we examine the pattern of these self-exciting activities, we find that it is very uneven. The user-supported sector is intensely self-exciting for one reason; the public-supported sector is much less self-exciting and when it is excited, responds to quite a different incentive.

The user-supported sector is excited by its own success. Its resources have to be used, its capital must be put to work, its machines must be kept busy, its newspapers must be filled, output must be kept up and up, if mounting overheads are to be carried. It is generally less disastrous to sell at a loss than not to sell at all. The public-supported sector, on the other hand, is not excited but (as it should be) relieved by its successes, and excited by its failures.[2] If a weighty effort brings the school-building programme or the health programme or the defence programme more nearly in line with aspirations, the next budget is likely to shift its priorities, even to abate its total demands. 'Success' does not generate more revenue or leave more accumulated resources waiting to be invested.

Broadly, in cybernetic jargon, feedback is negative in the public-supported sector but positive in the other.

There is, however, one other link between the two systems. The public-supported system is mainly excited by the imbalances created by the user-supported system. The user-supported system disturbs physical and social relationships. The demand for regulation falls on the public-supported system and so does the blame for failing to solve what may be insoluble problems generated by the user-supported system.

Within the user-supported system itself, there is another disparity to be noted. The increase in abundance has taken place in those goods and services which can be multiplied by mechanized and automated processes, not in those which involve personal service or personal skills. This concentration on goods rather than services is masked by the fact that many activities, classed as services, can be mechanized and automated. In America today, for the first time in human history perhaps, more than half the labour force are in 'service' industries. This is noteworthy. The fact remains that in New York it is much easier to get a television set serviced than to call in a doctor.

Briefly then it may be said that the user-supported sector is self-exciting, whilst the public-supported sector is not; that the System is set to produce goods rather than services and impersonal services rather than personal services; that it is much more responsive to individual wants than to collective needs; and that it powerfully resists the creation of any 'good' which can only be achieved by abating rather than redoubling activity.

When we look ahead, it seems clear that the linear progress which so many prophets envisage will challenge the System, in all these respects, in the order of its greatest weaknesses.

The growing GNP contains very different elements, growing at very different rates. At least five need to be distinguished.

The first includes all those extra resources which we need to generate in order merely to stand still – to keep the air no more polluted, the houses no more crowded, and so on. All these cost more yearly, merely to avoid regress. This, however, is inseparable from the second factor, which includes making the environment at least good enough to meet the minimum expectations – already frustrated and mounting – of those who cannot be ignored. This means doing much better than standing still.

The third element is the ever more costly capitalization of the productive machine which is to produce this rising GNP. The fourth is the ever rising expenditure on defence, space exploration and other such exercises.

None of these four activities produces any goods which an individual can choose and buy. Only the second produces any increment of 'good' which an individual can enjoy at all. Only the balance, the fifth element after these four have been satisfied, enlarges that field of choice which the individual exercises through the market and which, in Western countries, he has come to value so much. The question whether this fifth element will rise or fall – and for whom – can be decided only after a careful assessment of the other four, an assessment which is made almost impossible by the doubts which attend the fourth. But whatever the answer given, it will surely show that by far the biggest expansion will go into goods and services which are not chosen by individuals through a market but by public bodies through the political process.

Welfare economics has charted several classes of goods and services of this kind. They include those goods which, if supplied, must be supplied to all, such as lighthouses, sewers, and diplomats. They include goods which, though they benefit the receiver, are even more important to his neighbours, such as the treatment of infectious diseases; and their opposite, the negative good of being protected from harm from another's activities, as by his pollution of water or air. They include goods which only a government wants, like space probes, or which only a government is able and willing to supply, like the largest irrigation schemes; and negative goods of the same kind, such as proceed from traffic control and economic stabilization and the keeping of law and order. They include the preservation of goods which market valuation would destroy, such as open spaces in cities; the prohibition of goods which market valuation would create, like heroin; and the forced consumption of goods, like education, which some people might otherwise not choose, even if it were freely available. Many of the goods just listed can, of course, be supplied through the market; industry can build the roads, the schools and the lighthouses. What the market cannot do in this essential and expanding field is to elicit or restrain their appearance or declare their 'true' value by that process which was once thought to be the prerogative of the market.

Clearly then, one implication of the current trend is a huge increase in the load to be borne by the process of political choice; and the question arises whether the machinery for making these choices, on which Western societies pride themselves, will be able to support without radical change the additional load.

This is the subject of the next chapter. But before turning to it, it is convenient to examine some conceptual barriers which at present make these new political tasks even harder than they might be.

Let us first remind ourselves that nearly everything in the description which I have given of the System might be otherwise and in many other places is otherwise. It is an historical phenomenon, peculiar to a minority of the earth's inhabitants, rapidly changing and not widely copied. It is most unlikely that any now developing country will grow by an expansion of the private sector comparable to that which created the economics of Western Europe and America. No law of nature prescribes that productive activity shall be largely in the private sector or that user-supported activities (and their ever-increasing reserves of wealth) shall be beneficially owned by individuals rather than by public bodies or that governments shall derive their revenues largely by annually voted taxes. These attitudes have historical roots; many of them have arguable advantages; but they are none the less cultural artifacts, needing no less critical examination than those which are the more common targets of conceptual innovators.

Three attitudes seem particularly relevant.

The concept of competition already involves, in the philosophy of both public and private sectors, contradictions which demand resolution. Both still officially regard competition as good.

But competition is impossible unless competitors, ideally all of them, have unused resources with which to expand at each other's expense.[3] Unused resources, however, once assumed without question, are now held to be bad. The change is simply explained. In the old days unemployed labour supplied the elasticity for the competitive system. It was the main resource needed for expansion; it was usually there when wanted; and when not wanted, it 'cost' nothing to either sector, whatever its real cost. Since 'labour' – in other words, the majority of the people for whose benefit the whole affair is supposed to be going on – is no longer willing to provide the elasticity for the system, unused resources now mean plant and resources which are visible both on the ground and in the accounts.

The attempt to maintain a competitive system without relying on labour to provide some of the elasticity has naturally run into trouble. Full employment and a rising standard of living have been accepted as twin norms of policy; the suggestion that they may be even partly incompatible is deeply disturbing the British Left today. Far more radical incompatibility would appear, if the forecasters of increasing productivity are even roughly correct. There will not be enough work to go round. What work there is will require qualifications not possessed or attainable by a large slice of the work force which will exist at that time. Of those who work, only the highest placed will work exceedingly hard. The population of working age – it will no longer be a labour force – will divide into three streams; the over-working minority at the top, a featherbedded majority in the middle and an excluded minority at the bottom. I do not personally believe that this forecast will be realized for reasons to which I will return; but in so far as it is realized, it will make nonsense both of a government policy which aims at combining full employment with a rising standard of living and of a trade-union policy which aims at distributing the work available among all by cutting the hours of work.

A further tangle of out-dated assumptions confuses the concept of the market.

Markets are most convenient institutions. Some, notably the money market and the commodity markets, still retain an astonishing pitch of technical perfection. All have an important distributive function. But the market for goods and services retains to some extent, chiefly in America but to some extent even in England, a mystique which it no longer deserves as a mechanism for objective valuation. This helps to retain for it in our thinking a central place which it has long ceased to deserve. The goods and services provided by acts of political choice, though they multiply, are still too often thought of as regrettable exceptions to a general rule. In these fields we must reluctantly leave it to the political process to decide on priorities and within these priorities to decide for each who is to profit and who is to pay. But outside this suspect and subjective area *we know*. The market tells us.

This is no longer tenable. The economist's theory of the market was based on a number of assumptions which were accepted not because they corresponded with the real world – some manifestly did not – but because they were simple enough to handle and accurate enough to work in what used to be a substantial area of human activity. The free market in which the choice of consumers was supposed to adjust the products of competing producers was a market in which both consumers and producers were so numerous that no one of them could affect the outcome of the whole; and where consumers' wants were supposed to be fixed and uninfluenced by the market or indeed by anything else. Consumers were supposed to know their wants and to know how best to satisfy them, in any given state of the market. Producers profited and even survived only in so far as they could guess or fill the unfilled need better than their rivals.

This model worked well enough only in fields in which its basic assumptions were not too far from the truth. Notable among these are the assumptions of effective competition and of wants which can be taken as given. The field in which both hold has so narrowed as to be the exception rather than the rule. Competition has lost its mainspring of unused resources. Wants become increasingly a function of supply. In the market, as in politics, advocates of rival values appeal to individuals for their support and do all they can to mould these individuals' valuations to support them.[4] Nowhere outside the totalitarian world are their political choices manipulated so openly or so effectively as are their market choices in the Western world. In politics rival parties criticize each other, whilst the mass media criticize all. But in commerce mutual criticism of products is banned; only in recent years has the rise of consumer protection organizations subjected the commercial suppliers of goods and services to even the mildest informed criticism. The citizen has far more effective means to influence government than the consumer has to influence his economic masters.

We are in sight of a technology which would recreate a paradise for the economic man. A system of specification and testing would record on computers, centrally, reliable information on every product. A retrieval system would enable any inquirer anywhere to elicit from the central data bank particulars of all existing products in any field which concerned him, with the data needed for him to make any of those comparisons which the economic man was supposed to do in his head. This organization, though expensive, would be easily paid for by a levy on producers not heavier than their present advertising appropriations, and as these would no longer be necessary no additional expense would be involved. The consumers would be far better served with information than they are now; and if they behaved like economic men, producers of better mousetraps would be rewarded even more quickly than in the days when the merits of their wares had to be decided by personal inspection or even by personal trial and error. What would happen to our supposedly market economy and to all that depends on it if these supposedly classical conditions were restored to it?

But the main factor which displaces market choice by political choice is the increasing cost or benefit – usually cost – which flows from many market transactions to third parties and to society generally, in fields remote from the interest or even the imagination of the parties concerned. It is this which increasingly involves those multi-valued collective choices which are the stuff of politics.

Welfare economics tries with increasing sophistication to 'sum' the individual gains and losses resulting from the public creation of collective goods but does so largely still within the very unsophisticated limits of a false antithesis. *Either*, it is argued, some paternal dictator decides what is good for us *or* some process sums our own individual valuations of these goods and thus disentangles our preferences as the market does in its own area. The antithesis obscures the fact that our preferences between collective goods and individual goods and between one collective good and another, far more than between packets in a supermarket, are not given but are the subject of that mutual persuasion which is the democratic process. Democratic political leaders neither dictate collective goals nor seek to sum what they think individuals want.

The men and women of England who abolished slavery, created the educational system or gave women the vote were not acting on hypotheses of what the voters wanted. They were afire with faith in what people ought to want and in the end they persuaded their lethargic compatriots to give them enough support to warrant a change. American presidents, from Lincoln to Kennedy, do not speak with accents of enquirers seeking guidance about other people's preferences ... they criticise contemporary values, urge revaluation and appeal not to what people are thinking now but to what they ought to be thinking and would be thinking if they exposed themselves with sufficient sensitivity to the subject matter of the debate. A free society is one in which these initiatives spring up freely and in which men are free to espouse or resist them.[5]

Thus the increasing importance of 'collective goods'

magnifies the importance of political choice and thus of the political process. It is not the only influence to drive in this direction. For politics is concerned with power and the outstanding characteristic of our ever more crowded and more active world is the increasing power exercised wittingly and unwittingly by each over all. It is time to explore the proliferation of power.

NOTES AND REFERENCES

1. I have developed this distinction between the user-supported and the public-supported sectors in *The Art of Judgement*, Part II, especially Chapter II, London, Chapman & Hall, 1965; and New York, Basic Books.

2. It is, of course, true that investments in the public sector commit the future, no less than investments in the private sector. Buildings, staff and programmes, once established, make recurrent claims which are not easily reduced and which tend to grow. But this tendency, so constantly bemoaned, seems to me trivial when compared with the expansionist trend of the user-supported sector. The comparison is not drawn, only because expansion in the user-supported sector, however rapid, is deemed to be good, whilst expansion in the public-supported sector, however slow, is deemed to be bad. This value judgement is central to the mythology of the System.

3. I am indebted to Professor Adolph Lowe for pointing out that, in classical economic theory, one branch of industry, like one firm, may draw labour and resources from another, if its competitive position enables it to pay more, even though none have resources which are actually unused. The point is significant chiefly as a reminder of the gulf which separates the assumptions of classical economic theory from the realities of today.

4. As Professor Galbraith has so forcefully pointed out in *The Affluent Society*, 2nd ed., revised, Hamish Hamilton, 1969 and *The New Industrial State*, Hamish Hamilton, 1967. Also available in Pelican.

5. Vickers, G., *Value Systems and Social Process*, p. 46.

4 The Proliferation of Power[1]

Politics is concerned with power – its generation, distribution, transmission and exercise. Since wealth confers power and power opens avenues to wealth, there is a close connexion between politics and the subject of the last chapter. The subject was called political economy, before the market system, which is the study of classical economics, claimed an independent existence; claimed indeed to offer a rival and superior means of making collective choices through the automatic mediation of countless individual preferences.

We should not underrate the benefits that have flowed from this development. It has not only multiplied wealth; it has also mitigated the struggle for power. The stability of British institutions since 1688 has been due not only to a happy constitutional adjustment but also to the coincidence that increasingly since that date it has been possible to get and keep wealth and prestige through a channel other than politics. There is always room for an additional millionaire, never for an additional Prime Minister and seldom even for an additional Permanent Secretary. So the competition of business has muted the far fiercer competition of politics and lent the political system an adventitious stability.

I have shown reason to think that this era is passing. It is to be expected that the market system, mediating all those individual choices which it is calculated to excite, should build up an accumulation of collective choices by its own hidden hand and that these should clamour increasingly for the visible governance of political power. This none the less raises a basic political question. Can the political process, as any Western country knows it today, manage the increased volume and complexity of political choices which the next thirty years will bring to it? If so, by what growth, in what directions? If not, what breakdown will lead to what alternative? Even if these questions cannot yet be answered conclusively, to ask them now may improve the chance that they will find acceptable answers later.

The political process as Western societies know it has two ill-defined limitations, suggested by the words 'responsibility' and 'consensus'. These are the limitations which I explore in this chapter. I must give an unusually wide meaning both to political action and to responsible action.

I will define political action as the exercise of power over others; and responsible political action as action taken with regard to the expressed or supposed wishes or interests of the others whom it affects.

Political action in this sense covers the exercise of *all* power over others, irrespective of whether it be intentionally or even knowingly exercised. I shall speak of action as more or less political, according to its importance for others, relatively to its importance for the agent. Similarly, by *responsible* political action I shall mean action taken with regard to the interests of others, whether these others have any means of holding the agent to account or even of expressing their views. And I shall speak of action being more or less responsible, according to the weight attached by the agent to the interest of the others, relatively to his own.

Thus, in these terms, a wholly non-political action is one which affects the agent alone; and a wholly non-responsible political action is one which is taken as if it affects the agent alone, though in fact it affects others also.

These meanings are, of course, much wider than those usually implied. They are also loose. Almost any action has some effect on someone other than the agent. No formal standard exists to measure the relative importance for others of the more or less political, or the relative concern for others of the more or less responsible. None the less, I suggest that the terms are serviceable; and one of the services they render is to define two significant directions of current political change.

For many decades action in urban societies has been

growing more 'political', as their citizens become more numerous, more active and more crowded and maintain with each other a greater volume and variety of relations. It has also been growing more 'responsible', partly because the 'others' – and everyone is in some context an 'other' – finding themselves more affected, have found ways of insisting that their interests be considered; and partly because of an increased concern for others, which has emerged in these societies, not solely, I think, in response to these self-protective reactions.

According to this view, the growth of responsible government is only one aspect of the growth of a responsible society.

Political action, in the wide sense in which I am using the term, is of three main kinds. It includes, first, the unconsidered results on others of actions taken by an agent in pursuit of his own legitimate interests. In a world of multiplying relations, these increase in a way too familiar to need description. The urban citizen cannot take his car on to the road without restricting the freedom of movement of his fellow citizens and adding to the pollution of their common air. An increasing number of actions, legitimate in themselves, are deemed unacceptably damaging to others, and the would-be agent is required to curtail, change or abandon them, either by legal constraint or by the constraints of a shared social ethic.

Political action increasingly includes also the *considered* effects of private action on others, even though taken in an area formerly deemed to be adequately regulated by the market. The urban developer determines for some decades ahead how his fellow citizens shall use a particular area of increasingly limited land. So he also is increasingly subjected to the constraints of regulation by the public power.

Thirdly, and most characteristically, political action includes action taken by public bodies to meet those collective needs which the initiative of private agents cannot or does not supply. The growth of such action is attested by the proliferating agencies and departments of federal, state and local government, in fields such as education, health and welfare, transportation and urban development, as well as in the older fields of law and order.

Traditionally we associate the first two kinds of action with agents in the private sector, the third with public authorities. The distinction is becoming less exact and is already misleading. Agents in the private sector, whether individuals or corporations, do not always regard the public interest merely as a set of boundary conditions, to be accepted only as limitations. They increasingly share some positive concern in serving the public interest and include it among their criteria of success.[2] On the other hand, agents in the public sector have their 'private' interests, legitimate as well as illegitimate, which often collide with wider or different 'public' interests. Local authorities regard the interests of other or wider localities, much as private agents regard the interests of other private agents. Functional authorities feel similarly towards authorities charged with the performance of other functions. And all sorts of inner requirements and conveniences, administrative and financial, create a 'private' interest even for public corporations, not to speak of the private interests of their human constituents, who are just as human and just as private as anybody else, even though constrained by somewhat different roles.

None the less, the types of political regulation which we associate with the two sectors are valid, even though both types are usually involved in both sectors. One type is the reconciliation of individual interest with other individual interests or with a common interest. The other type is the reconciliation of many common interests with each other. Both are attempted solutions of essentially conflictual situations; and as action becomes more political and more responsible, these conflicts grow sharper.

They are aggravated by another factor that I have so far excluded. I have referred to 'the agent' as though powers of action and powers of decision were always vested in the same person. But of course they are not; they become ever less so. As policies, to be adequate, become wider in their scope, they involve more agencies in their operation, with different functional responsibilities at different levels of government. The policy maker must expect to rely on more and more executive agencies which he does not directly control. The executive must expect to be involved in the carrying out of many policies which he does not directly make. The difficulties of thus separating policy-making from executive responsibility in government are well known and still unsolved; the need to make action departments responsible to wider policy directives breeds conflict within the regulative machine itself.[3]

If the foregoing analysis is right, the task of government is growing more difficult, through changes which it cannot control and which show no prospect of abating. And these tasks grow more, rather than less, difficult through the need to perform them 'responsibly'. Deadlock or open conflict may in theory arise at any time – deadlock, where each of all the possible actions is unacceptable and can be frustrated by the group which would be most damaged by it. This situation can arise even where 'no action' is equally unacceptable to all; conflict, where even one group is not prepared to accept whatever action is determined. Such deadlocks and conflicts are always lurking possibilities, sometimes frightening realities. The course by which any modern society pursues its way is marked by crises, each of which is surmounted after delays in which such deadlocks and conflicts are somehow resolved.

'Somehow' covers a mixture of processes of great variety and obscurity. The configuration of power in the actual situation; the bargaining power and skill of the parties and their willingness to compromise; the ways in which they see the issues involved; and their (often forgotten) capacity to 'change the minds' of each other and themselves in the course of debate – all these are involved. There are differences in the way they are combined in different communities, even in the West – between USA and Britain, between Britain and France, even between USA and Canada. I am concerned here only with one aspect of this process, the strength of the parties' felt need to reach *some* acceptable solution – in other words, to preserve the consensus.

For the fact that 'government by consent' still takes place is due to a form of responsibility less conspicuous but not less important than the one I have explored. This is the responsibility of those affected to accept, *up to a point*, the exercise over them of private and public power, provided that decisions are reached and power exercised in ways socially and legally approved.

This responsibility, like the other, has its limits. These are the limits of the democratic consensus, the basic convention under which government is carried on. They are definable only when they break down; and they are then the subject of most bitter dispute. The right to rebel, to break the consensus, is, or used to be, a treasured democratic right; but the circumstances which justify it are always the subject of irreconcilable dispute. Each side's patriots are the other's traitors; hence the exceptional bitterness of civil war.

Even where the dissenters take no illegal action and refuse no legal obligation, their continued dissent involves both them and their fellows in combining two roles which may become intolerably inconsistent. The dissenters must concur in implementing the decision, whilst they continue to contest the policy; and the others must tolerate the continuance of debate on policy, however inimical this may be to its execution. Here again the limits of consensus will become visible only when they are overstepped.

The age-long struggle to make power responsible has hitherto been the struggle to secure the political rights of individual men. For several centuries in the history of this struggle, it seemed that the only corresponding responsibility on the individual was the responsibility to be brave and watchful in the defence of his rights. This is evidently changing. Liberty is no longer to be bought at a price so relatively cheap and simple as 'eternal vigilance'. The aim of the ancient struggle needs to be restated. It is 'to keep man the doer in the service of man the done-by, without frustrating either party in the process'. This casts an increasing burden of responsibility on the 'done-by', as well as on the doers.

The qualification implies new problems, with which we have yet to come to terms. Evidence of the need abounds. For example, man the doer is being subsidized by his government to inflict on man the done-by a form of supersonic air transport which man the done-by does not want and has good reason to dread. On the other hand, man the doer is failing to provide, for a large minority of man the done-by, an urban environment which man the done-by needs and wants and could have. The ancient antithesis between ruler and subject has been replaced by the antithesis between man the doer and man the done-by. And this finds no easy resolution through the fact that, viewed collectively, the doers and the done-by are one and the same. For in different contexts different men appear as doers and as done-by; and in terms of power and initiative, the doers are usually relatively few, the done-by relatively many.

What then are the responsibilities of man the done-by in a would-be self-governing society? They are two-fold as they have always been; to maintain with his fellows the dialogue which sets and changes the goals and limits of collective action; and also to take part or acquiesce in the action or inaction that results. These two activities make partly inconsistent demands and the inconsistency grows sharper, for reasons which are all too familiar.

The most obvious of these is the mounting rate of physical and conceptual change. Historically by far the most potent force in securing the responsibility of the doers and the acquiescence of the done-by has been habit. The dissolution of familiar situations – still more, the dissolution of familiar ways of seeing the situation – leaves both doers and done-by to reach new accords on how to see and how to value their common situation, as well as on what to do about it; and in this they are impeded by habits of thought and action which are no less strong for having become inept.

A further difficulty is the increasing complexity of these novel situations and the greater scale of space and time over which they can usefully be considered. Man the done-by – and often man the doer also – must guess or take on trust from others far more of the facts on which he must judge and act.

A third, less noticed but, I think, no less important difficulty is the increasing clash between economic and social interest, despite their close mutual relation. People want to live in a social context of human scale, even though their economic context is increasingly global. This is expressed in increasingly violent demands for cultural autonomy by sub-cultures within the political state. As an instrument of economic expansion, the organs of power, private as well as public, need very large, uniformly motivated populations. As instruments of social self-realization, on the other hand, they need to recognize and foster diverse cultural traditions.

So the tensions mount within the role of man the done-by. He has to suffer the exercise of increasing public and private power; for this is needed to create and preserve his livelihood. He has to entrust to others (in both private and public sectors) greater control over his well-being and his destiny, even though he knows, or should know, that these powers will be exercised in conditions of such doubt and risk that they are bound sometimes to be grossly misused. He must even support and encourage the doers in these massive exercises of power, especially in the public sector, which is most sensitive to public criticism and mistrust. The fact that he has, in the public sector, a limited choice of whom to trust does not make much easier his responsibility to accord to those in the seats of power sufficient support to enable them to do their job.

All this requires beliefs, deeply felt and widely shared by both doers and done-by, about the nature of the political situation, the goals of political power and the modes of political action.

But these beliefs are generated by the dialogue of the democratic process; and at times of doubt and change this requires radical questioning of accepted beliefs and daring innovations in accepted ways of analysing and valuing the situation, as well as new ways of responding to it. This in turn requires from all the participants tolerance of deviance, willingness to consider the unacceptable and to explore the shocking, to suspend judgement and to defer action until enough agreement has been generated. Nothing could be less apt to a time clamorous with needs and demands for collective action.

So each participant in the democratic dialogue must be aware of the frail, conditional consensus which alone makes possible anything that can be called government by consent, of his responsibility to maintain it, of the cost of breaking it. Yet he has still to maintain the dialogue which alone can keep man the doer in the service of man the done-by, fighting with weapons less controllable against interests more mighty for rights whose boundaries in daily life grow even harder to discern, whilst the costs of debate and delay become even more obvious.

The problems of mass democracy in the late-industrial age have scarcely yet been posed, let alone solved. The greatest among them may well prove to be the ancient task of preserving, between these narrowing limitations, that consensus which enables the search to go on. Since this consensus is a matter of faith and basic assumption, it needs to be explored with circumspection; yet not with inhibition, least of all in the United States, which attaches so much importance in its own two centuries of history to a revolution and a civil war.

What is felt to be a threat to the consensus may be either some action or inaction designed to thwart or change some formally legitimate exercise of power; or it may be a communication, questioning some element in the underlying assumptions and beliefs which is held to be beyond debate. These two are not so distinguishable as was once supposed; for every act is also a communication and is usually more potent as a communication than as an act. Even the grossest exercise of force, whether in rioting or in suppressing a riot, operates chiefly as the communication of a present and future threat.

This is, moreover, its intent. Even illegal acts, like illegal utterances, are none the less communications and are often intended to operate mainly as communications.

What then distinguishes a threat to the consensus from the surrounding stream of criticism, argument and trials of strength which constitute the democratic dialogue? Not that it is an act, rather than a communication. Not even that it is illegal, rather than legal. (A vast amount of criminal activity is felt as far less challenging to the consensus than some legitimate but radical protests.) It would seem that such threats are defined simply by being recognized as such either by the originator or his fellows or both. We know so little of the conditions on which political and social coherence depends that we cannot tell how these judgements of recognition are made. However they are made, they are 'facts' which tend to validate themselves.

Three contemporary issues in American life illustrate three forms in which the consensus may be strained, sometimes to breaking point. All of them have abundant historical parallels elsewhere; but in America, at the moment these words are being written, they can be seen together in the context of a modern industrial society.

Dissent over Vietnam expresses for many (at the time I write this) their rejection of the official view of world politics and of America's proper place in world politics. The advocates of this deviant view want to establish it in place of the official; thus far they are on common ground with the advocates of any other political change. What distinguishes some of them is that in the meantime they can no longer identify themselves with an America whose image is so much at variance with the image to which their personal loyalty attaches. What distinguishes others is that their fellows regard their protest not as criticism of a policy but as a sabotage of its execution. In either case, from one side or the other or both, the underlying consensus is felt to have been broken.

History abounds in such examples. In every country of Europe, in the last few centuries, men have been martyred, minorities slaughtered or expelled through similar breaches, sometimes generated by differences in dogma which today only an historian can understand – as perhaps tomorrow only an historian will be able to understand the slogans which divide us today.

Dissent about civil rights may equally express a wide variety of criticism; but for many it expresses their rejection of a social attitude which they find endemic among their fellow men about racial relations in the USA. Once again, for some of them this rejection is so radical that they feel bound to dissociate themselves from an America whose image is in this respect so grossly at variance with the image to which their loyalty is due. Others, for similar reasons, are rejected by their fellow citizens. The history of social reform is littered with similar examples.

A more radical though more amorphous threat to the consensus is implicit in the passive resistance offered by some of the young against taking over their cultural inheritance and its inherent values. This again may be expressed by illegal acts, notably the use of prohibited drugs, or by legal but dramatic flouting of convention. It may or may not express radical alienation from society; and it may or may not be regarded as such. But within this wide spectrum is a substantial body whose opting out is so radical that they regard themselves or are regarded as being outside the consensus.

This also is no novelty. One evening in February 1830 a crowd of young men, long haired and weirdly dressed, flooded the Comédie Française in Paris to support the first night of Victor Hugo's *Hernani* against the literary critics, shocked defenders of the classical tradition. They would have been at home in Haight Ashbury in 1967 (even to the fragments of old uniforms); and the Romantic Movement which so excited them had much in common with the protest movements of today. It too protested against the dominance of the rational – or perhaps against the narrow concept of the rational which was implicit in the orthodox culture. It too insisted on the primacy of personal experience. It too strained and sometimes broke the bonds of the consensus.

Of these three protests the first is focused on an aspect of public policy; the second on an aspect of social behaviour; and the third on an aspect of the cultural value system. Political, social and cultural criticism are endemic in every society in which custom is open to criticism. The art of governing – and of being governed – is so to shape the institutions and so to regulate the working of a society that it can contain the criticism which it generates. And it is here, I think, that the dilemma which I defined earlier will require a solution more rigorous than we are at present prepared to allow.

It is easy to conceive a state, even one so large and complex as the USA, united by a common culture so strong and uniform as to make both possible and acceptable the further proliferation of public and private power – but would so uniform a culture be tolerable or capable of generating and maintaining the dialogue needed for its further development? It is possible, though less easy, to conceive a state, especially one so large and complex as the USA, containing cultures so numerous and so varied as to accommodate human aspirations however diverse in conditions however changeful – but would such varied cultures provide a base for common political and economic activity on which all have come to depend? Any solution to this dilemma (if there is one) will, I think, be more costly than is commonly allowed. But the cost will have to be paid if man the done-by, in all his diversity, is to live and grow acceptably in the world which man the doer is making for him.

It would seem then that the political system to which Western powers are in principle committed depends on capacities and limitations which are either inherent in the individual psyche or produced by the social process by which each is humanized – a process which we know only in the historical forms in which we meet it and which in each society is conditioned by its own past. It seems clear, further, that the regulative power of our political systems is already being strained as never before and is going to be strained much further. It is time to turn from this brief survey of the trap to consider what we know of the trapped, and what we can hope of their capacities to transcend limitations which are essentially psychological and sociological.

NOTES AND REFERENCES

1. A translation of this chapter, under the title *'L'Art d'être gouverné'*, appeared in *Analyse et Prévision* July–August 1969, Tome VIII Nos. 1-2, Paris Sedeis.

2. I have developed this idea more fully in *Towards a Sociology of Management*, chapters 4 and 5, Chapman & Hall, 1967, and New York, Basic Books.

3. I have developed this idea further in *Value Systems and Social Process*, chapter 4.

Part II The Trapped

'Lords and Commons of England, consider what manner of men it is whereof ye are and whereof ye are the governors.' Milton answered his own question without the aid of social scientists, of opinion polls, or of personality tests. He could appeal to a shared model of man, no less than a shared model of Englishmen, far more precise and far more agreed than we can count on today – and very different.

It is the more important that a book like this should make explicit the model that it is using. 'The nature of the trap is a function of the nature of the trapped.'

5 The Personal World

The only organizing devices which are clearly identifiable in the contemporary human scene are human brains; so it is useful though sobering to review what we know of them and what we can expect of them. Since what we know relies so much and so inescapably on personal experience, I will express it as a personal view, though so far as I know it contains no scientific heresy. It does, however, involve three assumptions so strange that we do well to remind ourselves of them.

The cell from which I started carried, they say, complete instructions for the making of a man. Coded in the genes and reproduced with every cell division, these provide a model of decentralized control fantastic in its elegance and efficiency. Under their guidance, the cell produced in due course a biologically viable specimen, which still functions after more than seventy years. Its plan-governed activities still continue to repair and renew, with assurance born not of experience or instructions from higher authority or even of a comprehensive rule-book, but of ability to recognize deviation from an in-built norm.

Some months ago there appeared on the inner side of my upper arm a tiny patch of discoloured skin which soon formed a little sac containing a hard object. In due course the sac split open and rubbed away, leaving no scar and releasing no blood, but depositing in my hand a minute scrap of metal which had been blown into the other side of that arm in a military episode more than fifty years before. I cannot think that it was doing any harm; but the local cellular population recognized that it did not belong there and felt constrained to get rid of it, even though it took half a century.

Biology abounds in examples of this pragmatic ability to restore order, or the nearest practicable approach to order, however bizarre the disturbance and however unfamiliar the response required. We should not deserve to rely on it if we ceased to wonder at it, as Driesch wondered, when each of his sea-urchin embryos, if cut in half sufficiently early in its career, produced two perfect though rather small sea-urchins.

This, it now appears, is due to the staggering abundance with which information about *what ought to be* is encoded in every cell. I am not concerned here to inquire how deviation from this norm – a wound, for instance – excites adjacent cells to their work of reparation and guides them in their task. I would stress only that at this level regulation does not lack the first requisite of all regulation, a standard of what ought to be, by which deviation may be recognized and measured.

This standard regulates the whole system of internal relations which maintains the self-supporting organism; but this is only half the story. The creature depends equally on the external relations which its inner coherence enables it to maintain. For it is an open system, supported by exchanging matter and energy with its surround. Its form is more abiding than its substance. The regulation of these external relations depend on standards generated by a different process. The second assumption concerns this process.

Of all the organs which the cell reproduced in obedience to its in-built instructions, one, the brain and central nervous system, was itself capable of being further 'programmed'[1] by its own experience. Much is unknown about the working of this singular organ and much is probably unknowable; since it seems to be the only instrument of our understanding, it would be unreasonable to expect it fully to represent itself. But we have every reason to believe that it is the organ by which creatures have multiplied and organized their external relations and that its exceptional development in men accounts for the unique relations which they have established with their environment. These have hitherto contributed to the survival of the species and supplied an evolutionary explanation for the emergence of mind. Whether this development will continue to be useful is not to be assumed. The newly threatening course of these relations is part of this book's inquiry.

Among these external relations, communication with other men must from the earliest times have had special significance. For the enhanced human understanding of relationship even with the physical surround was itself based on a system of interpretation which was supplied by language and developed by human intercourse. Mind is a social artifact in the history of the species, no less than of the individual.

One result of this development was the emergence of human societies far more highly organized than those of other species. A primitive tribe living by hunting and food gathering is a system far more complex, both in its internal and its external relations, than any other species can exemplify and also far more capable of innovation and of accumulative learning. But another and parallel result was the emergence, within those societies, of individual personalities more complex and more highly differentiated. Language vastly increased the input of experience and the problems, as well as the possibility of organizing it; hence the diversity of the result.

It is useful to distinguish three kinds of experience, all contributing to the 'input' which the individual must organize as best he may; for the aspects most amenable to study by scientific method are those that matter least in the regulation of human affairs.

Earliest in time came the wave of sensory experience, through which I learned, like any other animal, to match my behaviour with the physical world around me, to get what I wanted and to escape what I did not, by interpreting as signals part of the incoming stream and learning to make signals which proved to be effective. But soon all this was overwhelmed by the experience of human communication, hugely amplified by the use of words, wooing, threatening, instructing, exhorting, encouraging, deterring. I admitted only a tiny and highly selected fraction of what flowed over me. Even so, my intake of experience from then on was to come far more in the symbolic form of words than in direct sensory experience; and these words were to mould my ways of receiving and interpreting experience, so that even the simplest biological facts of life, such as the needs for food, activity, repose and sex, were given meanings and values which they could not otherwise have had.

No communication has any meaning, except in conjunction with the setting of the receiving apparatus; just as a key's significance as a key is related to the lock it is designed to open.[2] But words are in some measure skeleton keys; and in some measure our receiving minds are skeleton locks. Each moulds the other. Talking and being talked to set going in me a circular process which was not only to magnify beyond measure my experience of relations with the world around me but also to define the ways in which I should experience it.

The language I learned contained an implicit order. It had nouns providing categories with which to distinguish objects, events, relations and even the more remote abstractions that I learned to make; adjectives describing their qualities and effects; verbs describing what they could do to me and I to them. These powerfully conditioned the kinds of order which I could distinguish or conceive. With their aid I ordered my own experience in my own particular way.

For these two streams of experience soon began to generate a third. I had to make sense of them, to reduce them to some kind of order. I experienced the inconsistencies inherent in this flood of instruction and interpretation, the conflicts between my own seekings and shunnings, problems arising in the management of fear, of time and of uncertainty. I developed strategies for living; not merely ways of acting but also ways of seeing and valuing which were to define and contain me and which I can revise the less as I learn more clearly to recognize them.

This was a normative process, imposing order on the flood of incoming experience by determining what I should notice, how I should define and value it and what I should feel constrained to do about it. By this process I built for myself the artifactual world in which I live, a world made to my measure and equally a world which moulds me. I can compare it with the worlds of others, in so far as communication enables me to understand differences, as well as to note similarities. But I cannot compare it with some 'real' world, common to all and objectively given, for that is both much more and much less than anybody's world.

There is a contrast between my biological development, confidently realizing its in-built norm, and my fumbling psychological development, realizing partially, slowly and by half blind and often inconsistent steps one among many apparently possible orders. The contrast lies partly between the mechanisms of control but much more significantly between the ways in which the standards of control are generated, preserved, transmitted and modified. Biological order (so far as we know) is encoded within the cell, transmitted by cell division and modified only by mutation and selective breeding. Psychological order, though its potentialities and limitations are biologically given, is established in each individual by the three forms of experience which I have described and is modified and transmitted by the same process of self- and mutual programming.

This contrast is much sharper than is commonly recognized. Biological order develops on an evolutionary time scale by a process of adaptation. Psychological order evolves on the scale of a human life span, by a learning process which is in almost every respect remote from biological adaptation. Grievous confusion results from the common practice of using evolutionary concepts to describe psychological development. Evolution is something that happens not to individuals but to populations or whole species. It does not depend on learning but on selection by an environment supposed to be constant at least over the immense spans which biological evolution needs – never less than many generations. The criterion of selection is simply survival – of populations and species, not of individuals. Learning, by contrast, is something done by individuals, within one life span; and one of its products is a host of often inconsistent criteria, among which survival even of the individual plays a role of varying and often negligible significance.

Here lies the most significant contrast between biological and psychological development. The biological standard, by which development is regulated, is self-consistent and does not change within the individual life span. The psychological standards which regulate thought and behaviour are multiple and conflicting; and a lifetime is usually too short to bring them into anything approaching a coherent, self-supportive whole. Learning what to want is the most radical, the most painful and the most creative art of life.

The individual at birth, let alone conception, is almost without sensory discrimination and is therefore almost closed to information. He has no power of coordinated response, beyond a few reflexes, and thus has most limited capacity of action; and he has no 'criteria' beyond a few un-coordinated impulses. Twenty years later he moves at ease in a conceptual world of great complexity; he possesses a large set of readinesses to respond to very varied situations; and he interprets his input of information and regulates his output of behaviour according to an elaborate set of criteria. Clearly a lot of learning has taken place in all the three sectors . . . learning which is still in progress, though its future course in each of these three dimensions is increasingly governed by its past.[3]

I have assumed that an organ biologically ordered, the brain, serves to generate and transmit all the standards by which personal life is regulated. The process is social, a mutual programming mediated by human communication; but the resultant system is personal. My personal world is unique to me. What little I know about it is learned by a process the reverse of that by which I learn about the personal worlds of others. For what I know of myself by direct experience I impute to them only by an inference which I can never fully verify (or conclusively disprove); whilst my knowledge of them, as I absorb it from experience and the social sciences, I can apply to myself only by pretending to an objectivity which can never be the same as that which I apply to them. Since I assume this to be equally true of others also, I must believe that every pair of human eyes looks out from a personal world different from every other in ways that can never be fully known. Still stranger, I must assume that every pair of human eyes looks out *into* a world which is equally personal, unique and private, if only because one of its constituents is, to those eyes alone, withdrawn from observation and communication but open to self-awareness and introspection.

What then of 'society' or rather of the manifold social orders, from families to nation states, from working groups to huge organizations, within which these personal orders arise and which they sustain? These too are systems more enduring than their constituents, proclaiming by their mere persistence the presence of regulative mechanisms responsive to enduring standards. We have to ask what are the mechanisms of regulation and how the regulating standards are set. But there is a more fundamental question – what is the relation between these ongoing systems and their transient constituents which seem so important to us because they happen to be our human selves?

The answers raise the third of those assumptions which I set out to explore in this chapter, not because they are unfamiliar but because their familiarity masks their strangeness. I have to assume that these personal and private orders, mediated by these individual brains, when linked through space and time in communicating networks, account not only for the pattern of individual lives but for the coherence of families and working groups, the individuality of village communities, the character of professions, the continuity of nations, the enduring yet changing patterns of religions and ideologies; that their present state contains all that human history has so far combined to weave and transmit and that their future activity alone will give to future history whatever form and whatever coherence it may achieve.

The relation between self and society has puzzled the West for two thousand years. The difficulty has been largely of its own making. For even in the Greek city-states of Plato's day, 'society' was already a complex and far from stable system. To reconcile the individuality of our personal worlds with the social structures which they compose and without which they cannot exist becomes harder as we ascend the scale of social organization.

The earliest form of social organization of which we have any certain knowledge and some surviving examples is a

ity of families living by hunting or fishing and food ering. Its numbers cannot exceed what its food supply can support. Its property cannot exceed what it can carry with it as it moves over its territory. Communities of this sort still exist today.[4] They pose few problems either to visiting anthropologists or to their own most speculative members about the relation of man and society.

The regulative standards of these societies are relatively stable and unchallenged, because they are the fruit of an experience which is not invalidated either by changes in the environment or by its own innovations. Each member entertains fairly complete and consistent ideas about the roles of all the others and his own in maintaining the social order; nor does he distinguish so sharply as Westerners do today the order of his personal world from the social order in which he is a participant. Food getting and distribution, the taking of collective decisions, the training of the young, the transmission of power – on these and a hundred other essential relations each new member of the society absorbs the common standards from all the others and plays his largely unconscious part in maintaining them, operating them and passing them on.

The process is only a partial analogy to that by which the pattern of biological order is transmitted but it is far closer to that pattern than any Westerner today can experience – except perhaps on the football field. For the coordination of players on a football field depends on conditions which today are seldom found elsewhere but which are deeply satisfying – hence perhaps the fascination of the game for both players and spectators. The players share an almost complete view of what is actually happening. They share identical standards for determining its meaning for them, both individually and collectively. They share a common repertory of responses for dealing with it, which gives them a common set of self-expectations. Equally, they know what to expect of each other and they have enough confidence in each other to act in the assurance that their expectations will be fulfilled. Given all these conditions, they exemplify decentralized control with almost biological perfection.

A primitive tribe is a comparable system. It is mainly

regulated by self- and mutual expectations, generated by long experience and transmitted by the voice of authority, speaking consistently through all its institutions. It is not, however, what we understand by an authoritarian society. It has its sanctions for correcting deviance – as all societies have – but these are seldom more than the expression of collective disapproval or ridicule, sanctions which are, of course, very powerful in a homogeneous society. It is often surprisingly tolerant of deviance. And it admits variations of personal character which seem to be as great as and identical with those to be found in a 'developed' society.

Simple agricultural peoples present a similar picture. They are simple in that the standards which govern their internal and external relations are clear and stable; but these may also be highly refined.[5] This in turn is due to the fact that their way of living, like that of their even simpler predecessors, is not so designed as to make itself obsolete. Old problems remain and tried solutions continue to solve them. The experience of one generation still serves to guide the next. A lifetime of experience is still an asset, not a disqualification for 'living in a changing world'.

In societies which still consist of groups of families, the relation of man and society presents no problem. We have reason to think that this was the mode of living even of our prehuman ancestors; so we may suppose that some traits appropriate to such a life have been biologically evolved in us. Having developed so striking a capacity for psychological and cultural evolution, we may of course be able to create and maintain stable social systems on a scale far beyond that of our biological predecessors; but we may assume that we shall encounter ever greater difficulties as we attempt syntheses further beyond those to which we are biologically adapted, and we cannot tell, except by experience, what we can achieve. We have every reason to try to regulate our affairs on the scale they now demand but no reason to suppose that we shall succeed.

Lorenz[6] has suggested that men, having become the most lethal of killers, are specially handicapped by the fact that, being naturally ill-armed, they never evolved devices for mutual protection such as have been evolved by wolves and other creatures that can kill at a bite or a blow. However this may be, it exemplifies the difficulties that beset us as we raise our tottering social structures into the unexplored regions of the human stratosphere.

When we consider the speculations of Western man on the relations between man and society, we see how closely tied they are both to his culture and to his civilization. For these have on the one hand so sharpened the separateness of the individual and on the other hand so extended the hierarchy of social organization as to raise perhaps insuperable difficulties in bridging the gulf between the two, either practically or conceptually.

One of the earliest theories to 'account for' society is the social contract. It appears in two forms – as an agreement for cooperative living, in which no one is 'subjected' to another: and as an agreement to be governed, in which the participants agree to subject themselves to a 'ruler' of some kind, to gain the benefits of law and order. In so far as the contract in either form is supposed to be made between 'a-social' or 'pre-social' men, it is obviously nonsense. Babies do not make contracts with their parents; and adults who have once been babies are no longer a-social or pre-social – though they may be anti-social, which is another matter. On the other hand, this contract in both its forms has clearly played a major part, among social men, in sustaining and extending society at different levels. The first operates whenever men combine to do together what they cannot do alone, as early settlers in North America combined to clear each other's land and build each other's houses, and as simple agricultural communities combine today in the major works of agriculture. This is the relation of the team and its members, the relation of the football field writ large.

In its other form, the contract of government is more important because it is applicable to much larger societies. Indeed, it is usually the last cohesive force to break, when the instability of such societies reaches breaking point. The individual in Western societies is dependent as never before on a society which is vulnerable as never before to massive dislocation, whether by acts of protesting or predatory minorities within or to threats from without or to failure of the confidence that maintains it. These threats, always present, become operative whenever they obtrude into consciousness, whether from an unusually violent riot, an unusually disruptive strike, an unusually arresting student protest or an apparently threatening gesture by another power. Whatever the trigger, it releases in favour of the contract of government the power of that vested interest in 'law and order' which is today by far the largest vested interest in any modern state – and with good reason. It seems likely to play a dominant part in the presidential election which, as I write (1968), is reaching its last stages in the USA. It has been and is the dominant force in support of De Gaulle's Fifth Republic. It is growing more conspicuous in Britain.

Another supposedly 'pre-scientific' theory of society is that it reflects an order inherent in human difference. The many are born to be ruled, the few to rule. This theory is so out of fashion that a writer risks his readers' forbearance by pointing out that it is in fact both true and important. Men differ in few respects more than in their wish and capacity for power. The struggle for power, whether in a Western state or anywhere else, is not and has never been a struggle of all against all. It is a struggle between that small, self-selected minority who choose to enter the lists. The vast majority – including at least its due proportion of able, intelligent and lovable people – are concerned only to be ruled as well as may be. The philosopher king, if not a contradiction in terms, is certainly the rarest bird in humanity's aviary.

Even so, the minority of power seekers is so large as to endanger any society which does not either mute their ambitions by its ethos or provide an expansible field for them. The chief political merit of the West's expanding economy, as I observed earlier, is that it provides for these characters a relatively safe expansion chamber outside politics.

Modern sociology, in so far as it ventures to describe large-scale modern societies, usually offers a systematic model in which the main regulative function is derived from the concepts of position, status and role. These have greatly clarified our understanding of the regulators which give society such coherence as it has and at the same time define the relation between the individual and society. The most obvious of society's regulators is the vested interest of every individual in the fulfilment of his expectations.

Every culture relies on a vast structure of mutual expectations and mutual confidence, which becomes visible only when it is shaken. On the simplest level this includes, for example, the assumptions that trains will run, that shops will have their usual goods for sale, that streets will remain sufficiently safe places to walk in. These and a thousand other expectations, though none is infallible, remain for long periods sufficiently reliable to support life based on the assumptions that they will be fulfilled. Behind these lie a second order of expectations, that countless individuals will continue to do what their roles require. All these expectations – and the multitude of others far more subtle which hold between individual man and man – are maintained by a constant stream of feedback, reinforcing compliance and restraining deviance. In this stream an essential part is played by self-satisfaction and self-punishment at meeting or failing to meet norms which have been accepted by the self and have thus become self-expectations. Where these exist, regulation is of course greatly refined and simplified. Mere information, without further sanction, is sufficient corrective.

This tissue of self- and mutual expectations is the basic regulator of society. It sets the standard of what ought to be, by which deviance is defined; and it is itself constantly on the move under the influence of the process which it mediates. It has been stressed, especially in the writing of North American sociologists.[7]

A European sociologist, Professor Dahrendorf,[8] recently inveighed against this model as overrating the extent to which such societies are or should be self-regulating through processes of automatic adjustment, and correspondingly underrating the role of conflict and of the constraints necessary to contain conflict. He offers an alternative model of which the central concepts are conflict and constraint. I think his criticism is justified. The liberal era has indeed underrated and often ignored the part played by conflict and constraint in the ordering of society; and I shall argue later that the greatest problem of Western societies in the next decades will be to contain a very high degree of conflict without losing those liberal principles which have enduring worth. But this does not seem to me to be a criticism of the systematic model as such. Of course every system depends upon constraint, in the sense that every deviance evokes some corrective action. Whether the corrective action be arrest by secret police, loss of a job, loss of promotion, disapproval by a peer group, loss of face or a sense of personal failure, it is none the less a constraint. It is of the greatest importance, in comparing societies, to note differences in the areas over which such constraints are applied and in their cogency. But in measuring cogency the attachment of formal, legal sanctions is only one indicator of constraint.

Equally, of course, conflict is endemic in every social system and at two levels which need to be distinguished. There is constant conflict between the forces of deviance and the regulators which seek to enforce conformity, whether in the fields of civil and criminal law, of ethical conduct, of artistic criticism and creation, of family relations or elsewhere. There is also, at least in Western societies, endemic and even more important conflict in the process by which standards in all these fields are set. To adjust these standards to each other and make viable compromises between them is part of the life of politics.[9] A more ambitious view of politics would attribute to it also a leading role in developing these standards, whilst maintaining them as a system sufficiently coherent to govern the life of a society. It is this last type of conflict which distinguishes modern from traditional societies.

These regulators, like any other regulators, may prove unequal to their task and may break down. The standards of what ought to be which set the system may become so confused that they cease to distinguish deviance; or they may become polarized in antagonistic forms. In either case, they will generate disruptive conflict. Some stability may be recovered later; but it is unlikely to be the stability of the status quo. But the fact that our societies are unstable to the verge of breakdown does not make the concept of system any less useful in understanding them and their pathologies.

It would seem to me, then, that all these supposedly conflicting theories of society make sense, once we recognize the huge spectrum covered by the different scales and types of human association and the difference between the cohesive forces which can be expected to work at each level. The key to this is to focus on the relatively small social systems which are the biological and psychological breeding ground of humanity. Within these groups the problem is how the individual personality is differentiated out; above them, the problem is how the individual is integrated in. The word 'social' loses its meaning as the mind's eye travels up this scale; the word 'political' loses its meaning as the mind's eye travels down. The political state is an attenuated *social* system. Simple societies and contemporary small-scale associations are only embryonic *political* organizations.

NOTES AND REFERENCES

1. I use the word 'programmed', here and later, reluctantly. To computer-minded people it will suggest no more than the programming of present, digital computers. To others it will suggest a view of mental operations which they will regard as 'mechanical' and therefore 'reductionist' and bad. I am driven to use this word, because 'learning' and, still more, 'teaching' are too narrow and specific both for the process by which we develop our minds and for the development which results. I describe more fully later (Ch. 7) both the process and the development which I intend to cover by the words 'programming' and 'programme'. To anticipate objection, let me insist now that I fully share the view of authorities quoted later that our more important mental processes are not digital and cannot be imitated by digital computers, however elaborate.
2. I owe this simile and much besides to Professor D. M. MacKay.
3. Vickers, G., *Value Systems and Social Process*, p. 119.
4. e.g., the tribes of Australian aborigines studied by C. P. Mountford, whose portraits and descriptions of individuals show vividly how varied and how familiar are the types of personality in a simple traditional society. Mountford, C. P., *Australian Aboriginal Portraits*, Cambridge University Press (Melbourne), 1967.
5. The legal system of the Barotse, as described by Professor Gluckman, will command the understanding and respect of any English lawyer. Gluckman, M., *The Judicial Process among the Barotse of Northern Rhodesia*, Manchester, The University Press, 1955.

6. Lorenz, K. *On Aggression*, Methuen, 1966.

7. Notably by Professor Talcott Parsons.

8. Dahrendorf, R., *Essays in the Theory of Society*, Routledge & Kegan Paul, 1968.

9. Henry Fairlie gives vivid expression to this in *The Life of Politics*, New York, Basic Books, 1968. His realistic and astringent account of what actually happens in politics, stressing the role of politicians as brokers of interests, has little to say of their role as formers of opinion. I do not know how far he would share the 'more ambitious view' of politics, as playing 'a leading part in developing standards, whilst maintaining them as a system sufficiently coherent to govern the life of a society'. His failure to acknowledge the function has been criticized by an English politician, Christopher Mayhew, in his book *Party Games*, Hutchinson, 1969.

6 Men without Roles

The large-scale societies of the West depend no less than earlier societies on the playing of roles; but changes on which they pride themselves have weakened the effectiveness of role-playing, whilst increasing their dependence on it. The divergence between the two is a threat both to individual integrity and to social coherence.

In traditional societies roles attach largely to positions defined by class or vocation. Even vocational positions, being usually attained either directly by inheritance or by traditional paths and being in either case secure, have a substantial social content. The craftsman, the herdsman, the farmer, the merchant and the priest, no less than the nobleman, are social as well as vocational roles, even where they are not determined by the accident of birth. Each is defined by a set of criteria, not limited to technical expertise, by which individual holders of the role may be judged to be performing well or ill – criteria widely shared by all holders of the position and by others whose approval matters to them.

Thus even in the Greek city-state an individual could be largely described by the social positions he held and assessed by his performance in them.

Two thousand years of history has eroded this structure in two ways.

First, access to vocational positions has been made increasingly contractual and has been opened increasingly to candidates of all classes. When Maine described this as the transition from status to contract, he obscured an essential feature of the change, which has been asserting its importance ever since. The nexus of rights and obligations which is transferred by contractual appointment to any position, public or private, in the modern world is far wider than the contract prescribes and extends far beyond the contracting parties. What is in fact transferred is a *social* position, with its accompanying status and role. The fact is obscured only by our reluctance to recognize the organizations of business and government as social structures. That such positions can now be transferred and even created by contract is a major social invention; but it has costs.

Several merits can be claimed for the innovation. It facilitates rapid growth and change; and, when combined with increased equality of opportunity, it multiplies the number of actors available for the new roles and so offers the hope that the players of roles will be more suitable and more competent than they would otherwise be. It also offers the individual a wider choice of activity and human relationship and thus more scope for self-expression. The high values set on these achievements – on growth and efficiency in the larger systems, on choice and self-expression in the personal system – are artifacts of Western culture which I believe to be overrated, but I will take them for the moment at their face value.

These positions are the most important that our society has to offer, but they are also transient and liable to be taken away at short notice by unilateral action. They thus give rise to anxiety, especially in industrial relations, which is only now being recognized. Even when this is relieved, the vocational role which is transferable by contract has been largely emptied of its social content. The rise of the professions is a significant exception. But in general Western man is less fully described by his vocational role than a man in a traditional society, and still less precisely evaluated by being described as a good or bad player of the role. The market economy offers him its consolations as an individual, but depreciates his vocational status. Automation carries the process to its conclusion by making most of us more significant as consumers than as producers.

Class roles have been even more thoroughly eroded, partly by the incidental effects of the market economy, partly by the ethically-charged drive for political equality, partly by a religion which belittled the secular supports of social man in the course of preparing him to meet his God.

What then is left in terms of which a man may be described and evaluated by himself and others? Has he been liberated or reduced to vacuity? Many, including most sociologists, would insist that man – or at least Western individual man – is and ought to be more than a complex of roles; or ought at least to have the chance of being so. The crisis of identity is the price for which true individuality is bought. No price can be too high.

This view seems to me a product of that falsely heightened antithesis which Western culture has drawn between the individual and society (p. 77) and which is so passionately expressed in Professor Dahrendorf's book. The responsible, 'inner-directed' man, who can be 'true to himself', even against every social pressure, is himself a social type playing a socially recognized role. The kind of responsibility that he shows is attached to the role of being a man in that culture, or claimed by him as proper to that role, as other role-players change and extend the roles they are given. It may be convenient to keep the word 'role' for the expectations attached to more specific positions but the importance attached to separating role-playing from 'being oneself' seems to me a symptom of social pathology. Is not a person a 'persona', a character to be played 'in character'?

When an existing order becomes too confused, too lacking in authority for its roles to have their ancient meaning, men, especially rebellious men, look elsewhere for their significance. Some may find it in a world of strictly personal relations or even in a self-structured inner solitude, but others will create new roles, in opposition to the status quo. It is significant that the only clearly new human type to be evolved in England in the last one hundred years is the trade-unionist. Here is a role covering a wide area of human behaviour, in which a man's performance can be described and judged good or bad by others and himself according to standards shared at least by fellow trade-unionists. The 'good trade-unionist' is – or was – an admired type not much less comprehensive than his immediate predecessor the gentleman, whom he may soon follow into the limbo of confusion. It is too soon to tell whether any of the newer protest groups will generate so lasting and comprehensive a persona.

Clearly a society so dependent on role-playing as Western societies are must replace its old class and vocational roles with others besides roles of protest. Such roles are as yet hard to identify.

In communist countries and even in some countries of 'the third world' the role of the citizen has recovered its significance. In the West it has not – though the adjective 'un-American' could hardly have a meaning if simply 'being American' were a wholly vacuous role. It is more common, in the West, to seek both variety and security in the context of multiple roles, stemming from membership of numerous self-selecting groups, often widely diffused in space, as is the scientific community.

The concept is important, but it is not, I think, enough to meet the needs of the situation. Both at the personal and at the political level, increasing weight is falling on the role of the citizen. All urban societies have been limited by what they have been able to achieve in this direction. Most have been ultimately destroyed by failure to elicit and maintain in their individual citizens a set of self- and mutual expectations sufficiently strong, shared and appropriate to preserve the coherence of the system.

These expectations only incidentally guarantee rights. Their primary function is to build-in responsibilities. Rights do not make a role; they are at most ancillary to the status which it carries. Responsibilities, not rights, give meaning to personal and political life. This is why declarations of rights are usually so otiose. A declaration of responsibilities implies far more clearly the conditions needed to attain the rights and the individuals on whom they fall – which usually includes those who claim the rights. They establish not what should be in the future but what should be felt now. Though they do not state a programme of action, they define a resetting of actual regulators. That perhaps is why they are not used.

The greatest disparity visible in the Western world is the disparity between the least that its continuance requires of the citizen and the most that it expects. The purposes of society require increasingly cooperation extended over wider fields of activity and longer spans of time – the sort of activity which at the cellular level is secured by the common standard of higher-level order which is built into every cell. The West views with horror the attempt of totalitarian societies to establish similar norms; but it neither has nor seeks to find any means to provide any similar assurance in the regulation of its own affairs and it has as yet no reason to assume that such regulation is possible, so long as the higher level order which its components are to seek is itself ill-defined; self-contradictory or too transient to be matched by action. It is certainly lacking now. Hence the paradoxical dilemma into which the Western world is moving, as it grows less controllable with every advance in the techniques of manipulation and less predictable with every advance in the technique of information handling.

The difficulties of the West both in maintaining the large-scale societies which it has built and in finding a place in them for 'the individual' are perfectly understandable but they are not soluble as they stand. Both the concept of society and the concept of the individual will have to change. Both are in fact changing.

We are becoming more aware that 'the individual' of whom the social tissue is woven is not conveniently to be regarded as an organism contained by its skin,[2] but rather as a system, consisting of two sets of relations, each of which is perhaps indefinitely extensible. One set comprises the internal relations, psychological as well as physiological, which give him whatever integrity he possesses. The other comprises the external relations which link him to his surround and especially to his fellow men. He extends outwards as widely as his interests and his sympathies can carry him, on the wings of communication, especially mutual communication with other human beings. He can be described only as one term in a host of relationships, the other terms of which must be sought elsewhere. Yet these relationships grew with and depend on the inner integrity which enables him to sustain them. Psychologically, as well as physiologically, he exemplifies the pregnant dictum of Claude Bernard that the stability of the *milieu*

intérieur is the condition of free and independent life. Y
life which this stability makes possible is a life of external interdependence.

Our ideas of state and society equally await and begin to receive clarification. The conceptual tools are available. We no longer wonder whether, why or how 'a whole' can be more than the sum of its parts. We can recognize and describe systematically related things and events as being 'wholes' in various degrees, for various purposes, over various periods of time and within various conditions. We can distinguish types of system according to the principles by which each is regulated; a heap of stones, a candle flame, a river, and a rabbit are all in some respects 'wholes which are more than the sum of their parts', yet they vary widely in their types and degrees of 'wholeness' and none of them exemplify the more important processes by which human and social systems are regulated. We can distinguish systems made up of a whole hierarchy of overlapping sub-systems, each level exemplifying a different kind of order. A modern nation state is a system so complex as to demand description not only at many levels but in many complementary dimensions. Its political, economic, social and legal structures, closely linked though they are, need separate though complementary analysis still too complex for our attainment. But we are conceptually equipped to understand them at least in principle.

This systematic view brings into place another theory of society – or of the state – which has had a troubled history and still awakens strong emotions. We may call it the organismic theory. Individuals are clearly humble constituents in a massive pyramid of sub-systems, which today seem to culminate in the nation state. Why should not the individual be regarded simply as a constituent in one of these larger entities, whose life, however precarious, is likely to be at least a little longer than his own? Why should not his significance be seen simply as participation in the life of an organic growth so much greater than himself?

This view of society generates in the West today hysterical resistance, for reasons which are mostly bad; yet the view, at least in the extreme form in which we have learned to fear it, deserves to be resisted, apart from the fact that the greatest crimes in history have been committed in its name within living memory.

In the first place, it implies that we must choose between rival views of the human predicament or at least give permanent predominance to one viewpoint; whereas in fact we need to use an indefinite number of viewpoints, giving each the predominance that our current purposes demand for it. I deal with this more fully in the next chapter, when describing reality as an inexhaustible composition of complementary views.

Secondly, it confuses state and society in a way which we begin to recognize but cannot yet untangle. It seems to me quite impossible that the political state on today's scale can ever become coextensive with the social matrix within which individuals find their identity. So I can see no hope of satisfying the passionate current demand for direct individual participation in political decisions. The same difficulty seems to beset the equally passionate urge to transfuse large-scale economic institutions with personal participation in 'decision making'. Somehow accommodation must be reached, rather than identity achieved, between the political and economic institutions which sustain a viable public order and the social fabric which gives life its meaning.

Thirdly, there is much evidence that systems composed of large aggregates of human beings are not capable of the higher forms of human achievement. I see no means of *proving* that the systems which we individuals compose do not possess will or even consciousness in the same sense that individual humans do – that expressions such as 'the general will' and 'the national consciousness' may not be more than metaphors. But if they are, their achievement gives us no reason to respect these faculties even as much as our own.

In any case, the personal level is the level at which we happen to be. Innovation and conservation, revolution and evolution, the transmission and transmutation of experience (however determinate these processes may be) depend on the working of human brains and the communication and actions of individual human agents. It is individual men, however closely integrated, who feel, act, suffer, enjoy, aspire; who talk, write, persuade and are persuaded; who coerce, resist and rebel. The personal is the level at which they live. It is no cultural artifact.

This however does not excuse either the contempt with which the West views traditional societies or the hostility with which they view those so-called totalitarian states, which attempt – no less in the interest of 'the individual' as they conceive him – to integrate state and society on the scale of today and which are proposing and trying out alternative solutions to common problems. The West is not being so successful in its own solutions that it can either disregard the course of alternatives or condemn those happy peoples for whom the problems do not arise. The individual as the West conceives him to be is a creation, perhaps the supreme creation of Western culture – no less so because he is making a world in which he cannot bear to live. I have touched on some of the historical causes which produced the Western individual and turned him into the Western individualist.[3] I will not elaborate them here. I would only insist that we should not mistake for laws of God or nature the cultural values of the world's most unstable systems.

NOTES AND REFERENCES

1. The issue is most perceptively discussed by Professor Dorothy Emmet in *Rules, Roles and Relations*, Macmillan, 1966, especially chapter VIII. It is greatly clarified, I believe, if we distinguish between those role-expectations which are attached by society and those which derive from the behaviour of the role-player himself. Those who rely on him as doctor, employer, father, can appeal to a standard socially set of what is expected of *any* player of that role. But within these expectations, they can appeal to others generated by the past performance of the role-player himself. The greater the discretion which the role allows, the greater is the range over which those affected might complain – 'Though what you have done is within the range of what our society expects of *any* player of this role, it is outside the range of what you have led us to expect of *you*'. At the extreme, what we expect of A, simply as A, is based solely on what A himself, by his past behaviour, has invited us to expect of him – a completely individualized role, but none the less a role. For A himself the distinction is even slighter. For if he conceives 'being himself' as making a

coherent personality, the self-expectations which he derives from accepting his social and functional roles are no different in character from the self-expectations imposed by his idea of himself.

2. More exactly, we are becoming more familiar with the curious pair of facts neatly summarized by Professor Gorn – 'we spend the first year of our lives learning that we end at our skin and the rest of our lives learning that we don't'. Gorn, S., 'The Individual and Political Life of Information Systems', in E. B. Heilprin et al. (eds.), *Proceedings of the Symposium on Education for Information Sciences*, Warrington Va., Spartan Books, 1965.

3. I have done so more fully in a paper 'Individuals in a Collective Society', published in Ewald, William R., Jr (ed.), *Environment and Change, The Next Fifty Years*, Indiana University Press, 1968.

7 The Human Context

In the last chapter I explored the relations between the personal world of individual experience and the social world which these individuals compose and on which they depend. I will now extend this inquiry to cover the relation between personal experience and the whole of that 'real world out there' which we commonly assume. This relation has engaged philosophers in controversy for two thousand years (including more recently philosophers of science) and I shall try to do no more than state those of my assumptions which are relevant to this book. I am aware that some of them are not – or at least not yet – orthodox.

The most striking feature of men, when compared with other animals, is not their ingenuity in doing – that 'goal-seeking' of which we have heard too much – but their capacity for knowing where they are. They can represent to themselves what I will call their contexts – all those manifold relations with the world around them which they pursue and on which they rely and which help to define their meaning to themselves and others. These include not only the private contexts of individuals at home, at work and at play but also the public contexts which concern both statesmen whose roles engage them personally and every citizen who feels himself personally concerned.

I have in mind the power of conscious reflection which enables us to represent to ourselves our relations with people and events and the relations of others which involve us. This enables us both to 'understand' – or perhaps misunderstand – them and to exercise judgement about them by comparing them with standards at which we have somehow arrived, of what we expect or desire or think right or acceptable. It thus affects our attitudes towards these relations and helps to determine what they actually are.

These representations – and this is a strange and most important point – include the dimension of *time*. We can represent to ourselves the real or hypothetical course of events, past, present and future, and the engagement of our hypothetical selves. It is a limited and fallible instrument, supported by subconscious processes which we may never be able to identify, and is far too weak for our present needs; but it is none the less potent and astonishing.

This faculty is, of course, very useful in deciding what to do, though this is not, I think, its most important function. Rehearsing possible futures on the stage of the mind, we can play out a dozen alternatives, based on different assumptions, including the assumption of different interventions by ourselves; and we can defer decision until their probable outcomes have been anticipated and compared. This procedure relieves trial and error of its usual costs and extends its use far beyond its normally narrow range.[1] Having rehearsed some possible future where the curtain falls on disaster, we have only to dismiss the phantom actors and rewrite the script.

Knowledge gained from such an exercise is sometimes called 'feed-forward', to distinguish it from the feedback of actual experience. In all deliberate human action, feed-forward plays a far larger *direct* part than feedback. The signals of match and mis-match which alert our regulators are generated on the stage of the mind, usually by representations of the future.

Feedback is none the less incessant and indispensable; but it serves a different purpose. It monitors our representation of our context, confronting every expectation, as it matures, with the actuality to which it may or may not correspond. It corrects – or at least criticizes – not only unsuccessful actions but, much more often, inept appreciation.

This control may operate at subtle and sophisticated levels. Suppose that in conversation the other party answers me 'angrily'. If this corresponds with one of the possible responses which my representation of his state of mind would lead me to expect, I am not surprised – but I am informed, for I am confirmed (perhaps wrongly) in that view of his state which makes sense of his response. If, on the other hand, I am surprised, I am still informed, though much less positively. I am told only that something is wrong with my appreciation of my context. I shall be led to wonder why my communication meant something to him which it did not mean to me.

More commonly, communication is expressly directed by the parties to it to comparing and bringing into conformity their appreciation of some context common to them all. This is the object of almost every rational argument in politics, business or private life. This again immensely extends the capacity for common action, which would otherwise be limited to situations such as the football team already described (p. 78), where the whole complex of 'contexts' is visible to all. It also extends, reciprocally, the power to communicate, since the understanding of communication depends on the possession of a shared viewpoint – as distinct from a shared view – of the matter under discussion.

This world of represented contexts is, I suggest, the world in which we effectively live. It is our supreme mental achievement. Most of our communication is directed to developing it, revising it, trying to reduce its inconsistencies, to test its accuracy and to extend its scope.

I will call it our appreciated world.[2]

The appreciated world is selected by our interests; for only some interest would lead us to notice any of its constituents. Of course, we have many contexts which we fail to notice. We of the West, for instance, had been polluting our air and water for several decades before this aspect of our relations claimed our attention. These neglected relations force themselves on our attention in time and thus become part of our appreciated world; but we may be sure that at any time important aspects of our relations are hidden from us, because we have not noticed them. At the personal level, we often notice in our friends and especially in our children these distressing discrepancies between their 'appreciated worlds' and aspects of the real world which they are unaccountably ignoring. They often notice the same in us.

This appreciated world, thus limited, is given form by our expectations. For it is these which, matching or mis-matching the unrolling stream of events, confirm it or call it into question. Matching, no less than mis-matching signals convey important information. They reassure us that our appreciated world is sufficiently in accord with the real world to be serviceable. They thus minister not only to the assurance of our actions but to the assurance of our lives. They make us feel at home in our appreciated world. (This is a major function of ritual and ritualized response, such as formalized greetings and conventional social behaviour.) The mass media of communication, in addition to more familiar disservices, render one which has not yet been charted and which in any case they could hardly avoid. By recording only the newsworthy, that is, the unusual, they radically alter the proportion between match and mismatch in the stream of our input and make the world seem even more unexpected than it actually is. How much this contributes to our anxiety and confusion we have no means of knowing.

Our appreciated world is given meaning by our standards of judgement, ethical, aesthetic, political and other. However these standards are generated and changed, there is no doubt that they give meaning to our experience. What happens – or might happen – is compared not only with our expectations but with this battery of standards by which we judge it to be welcome, important, acceptable, good, right or the reverse.

I thus conceive our appreciated world as carved out by our interests, structured by our expectations and evaluated by our standards of judgement. I find it confusing to give the word 'values' any narrower meaning than will comprehend interests and expectations, as well as standards of judgement. Without some 'standards' we could not notice anything at all – nor did we, when we lay in our cradles, before the whole build-up began. I have already stressed that 'standards', 'norms', by whatever name called, are fundamental to any kind of control, biological, psychological or sociological. The generation of multiple and partly conflicting standards is the distinguishing mark of man and their management is his human business.

'Values' in this sense discriminate and select facts, as well as give meaning to them. The antithesis between facts and values which has haunted Western science and philosophy for so long is due, I believe, to a radical misunderstanding of the meaning of both, to which I will return.

The appreciated world, as it grows, organizes our further experience and mediates our communication, as well as guides our actions. It is an hypothetical world, in the sense that it is largely built up on hypotheses, more or less developed, about how and why things happen as they do. It is also hypothetical in the sense that it is never completely validated, much of it is highly uncertain and some of it may be and may remain radically, undiscoverably and irremediably wrong – if only because it is sometimes ahead of and sometimes behind the constantly changing 'realities' that it selects and interprets. When events are inconsistent with it, they seldom throw light on what is wrong with it; feedback is often no more informative than the return of an undelivered letter. Though personal, it is a social construct; it would barely exist but for human communication. It is the major social, no less than the major personal, creation.

Above all, the appreciated world is both a *composite* and an *inexhaustible* world. It is composite because it is composed of views seen from different viewpoints, which cannot be simply added together. It is inexhaustible because these viewpoints may change and multiply without any obvious limit. We can see our surround as a source of support, a field of opportunity, a multiple threat, an intellectual puzzle. We can see ourselves acting and suffering simultaneously in a score of different roles. Each view selects its own relevant facts, in relation to its own relevant 'values'. Each view needs to be described from its own viewpoint, sometimes in its own language – as a sociologist, a rioter, a bystander and a policeman *need* to give different accounts of the 'same' riot. Accounts given from the same viewpoint may be more or less subject to ignorance and error and every effort is needed to make each conform to 'the facts'. But the differences between them are due not only to ignorance and error but to a difference in viewpoint which, by making different facts and values relevant, ensures that the resulting accounts will at best be neither conflicting nor cumulative but complementary.

The expectations which order our appreciated world are rules derived from regularities which we abstract from experience. As a simple example, to sighted creatures whose life-span is measured in years, one of the most conspicuous regularities of nature is the alternation of day and night. This dramatic but regular change soon becomes recognized as a pattern, so that departure from it, as in an eclipse, becomes an alarming deviation. Except in low latitudes, another change is conspicuous, comprehending the first in an ampler pattern – the cyclical change in the proportions of light and darkness; and from this in time is abstracted the pattern of the seasons. To measure this alternation with sufficient precision is an early scientific achievement of the agricultural epoch, making possible the predictions involved in the sowing and storage of grain; but the pattern is sufficiently gross to be derivable from ordinary experience, given sufficient exposure to it.

The abstraction of rules from regularities like these is an example of that capacity for *pattern recognition* on which we rely not only in everything we do but in building the representation of our manifold contexts within which we live. This is the process of discovering order in – or imposing order on – the environment, which science has carried so far.

Not all the aspects of our environment are equally predictable. Rain and wind over the British Isles can be forecast, even by modern meteorology, only roughly a few days in advance. None the less, human experience, without benefit of any science, abstracts some useful generalizations – for example, that winds are not likely to exceed a given force or rain a given intensity and duration or floods a given height or annual rainfall to stray outside given limits – rules of which, in an old legal phrase, 'the memory of man runneth not to the contrary'.

These two kinds of regularity have been developed by Western science into its imposing structure of general and statistical laws.

Both science and common sense can contribute more than general and statistical laws to our understanding of where we are. A meteorological map, for example, shows variations in barometric pressure as a *system* of depressions, ridges and so on, moving and generating movements which will reverse them. The direction and force of the wind in an area over a period is represented as largely a function of these pressure gradients, of their movements and the speed of their change. The actual state of the field, still more its future changes, are not accurately known and perhaps may never be, but the concept serves to model the process and thus to give both a better understanding of what is and a better forecast of what will be.

Men without benefit of science were familiar with such systematic relations – often more familiar than Western men are now. The relations between the size of a pastoral tribe, the number of its animals, its maximum rate of movement and the pasture available are systematic relations. Pastoral tribes must have been well aware of them and of the relative costs of the different ways of keeping them in balance.

Men in their dealings with men create and recognize another kind of regularity – rules of their own devising, imposed and accepted consciously and unconsciously. The only reason why men are by and large more predictable than the weather is that they are *concerned to be predictable*; concerned to meet each other's expectations by accepting common self-expectations. This web of mutual expectations, which I described in the previous chapter, creates an order of which the regularities obey neither general nor statistical laws. They do not even show the regularities to be observed in simpler systems such as the weather. They evolve by an historical process which is neither reversible nor repeatable, because it generates those constantly changing standards to which I have referred and in consequence is constantly resetting its own regulators.

The description which I have given of the way in which we learn to appreciate our contexts is not, I believe, inconsistent either with common experience or with accepted views about knowing and learning, so far as they go. Yet it may seem to run counter to the deeply ingrained assumption that knowing is or ought to be an activity independent of any kind of human views or values; that these intervene only to distort or obscure our knowledge of 'reality as it really is'. To cast doubt on this may seem to question the 'objectivity' of science and the whole heritage of assurance which has been built on it.

I think this is mistaken; and I devote the next chapter to showing how in my view the whole empire of science is contained within the appreciated world – and what, in the process, it has done to our appreciative system. Before passing on to this, I will define a little more clearly the terms which I am using to describe both the process and the result of the process which I call 'appreciating', a word which I use because I want to escape from what seem to me the unduly narrow connotations of our ideas of knowing and of learning and from the distinction between them.

To account for the appreciated world – which is, after all, one of the most assured facts of our experience – I postulate that experience, especially the experience of human communication, develops in each of us readinesses to notice particular aspects of our situation, to discriminate them in particular ways and to measure them against particular standards of comparison, which have been built up in similar ways. These readinesses in turn help to organize our further experience, which, as it develops, becomes less susceptible to radical change. Circular relations of this kind are the commonest facts of life, though we are handicapped in accepting them by our long conditioning to the idea of causal *chains*, linearly linked in time. Since there are no facts, apart from some screen of 'values' which discriminates, selects and relates them, just as there are no values except in relation to some configuration of fact, I use the word appreciation to describe the joint activity which we call knowing and which we sometimes suppose, I think mistakenly, to be a separable, cognitive activity which is 'value-free'. Since these readinesses are organized into a more or less coherent system, I speak of them as an appreciative system. I sometimes refer to their state at any point of time as their appreciative setting and to any act which expresses them as an appreciative judgement. The appreciative world is what our appreciative system enables us to know.

NOTES AND REFERENCES

1. It is not always realized how small and trivial is the range of experience in which we can learn from trial and error. How often do we have the opportunity to repeat an experience in which nothing has changed, except our learning from the one before? The maze-running rat is grotesquely un-typical of the problem-solving human.

2. I have developed this formulation in *The Art of Judgement*, Chapman and Hall, 1965, and New York, Basic Books, 1965, and in *Value Systems and Social Process* (already cited).

8 The Scientific Distortion

Science has vastly helped to order and extend our appreciated world but it has not led us out of it into an 'objective' world, independent of all human viewpoints and values. It too has its viewpoints and its values. They can usually be taken for granted but they should not be forgotten. They are indeed a major contribution to our appreciative system.

Science contributes first the faith that the real world out there is regular; and that it is knowable, to an extent which only experience can decide, by the method of science. It contributes, further, a method which, I have suggested, is only a rigorous extension of the method by which most of our knowing is gained. It contributes finally an attitude, born of its faith and its method. All three have powerfully affected our appreciative system as well as changing our appreciated world. They need to be considered separately.

The method, fruitful as it has been, has limitations. It is limited first by the kinds of subject matter to which it is applicable. It is no accident that its first successes were achieved in astronomy, where the regularities of the heavenly bodies are conspicuous, undisturbed by our interest in them and sufficiently enduring to abide an indefinite series of observations; whilst its greatest later successes have been in the fields of physics and chemistry, where relatively stable (or identically repeatable) atomic and molecular systems will equally abide an indefinitely extended series of strictly comparable experiments. These conditions cease to hold when the object of attention is part of an historical process.

When the objects of its attention are men and societies the method is further limited by the fact that much of our knowledge of these is inescapably drawn from a source which is not open to physical scientists and which would horrify them if it were. All the words in any language which refer to human experience have meaning only in so far as those who use them have themselves had the experience to which they believe those words to apply. They know what it is to be human as they know nothing else; and they credit each other with thoughts and feelings similar to their own or defined by reference to their own, until experience leads them to revise these assumptions. The knowledge on which they rely in this field is thus differently derived, differently experienced and differently validated, in so far as it can be said to be validated at all.

This last limitation does not exclude science from the study of human affairs and many social scientists would say that I have exaggerated it. But the method by which science escapes this limitation imports limitations of its own. It is the method of abstraction. There is, of course, nothing unusual about abstraction; all acts of appreciation are dependent on abstraction. But it is questionable how far, in the psycho-social field, an abstraction can develop in scientific thinking which does not influence or even supersede the models of general appreciation. The economic man, we are assured, was not intended as a model of man but as an abstraction representing some aspects of human behaviour which are regular enough to support predictions. But the appreciative system needs models for its symbolic alchemy and the economic man in his time has profoundly influenced the behaviour which he was supposed merely to predict and has thus supplied himself with a good deal of bogus self-validation. And even now that he has ceased to serve very well even as an abstraction, he retains in the appreciative system of the scientists who created him a reputation based largely on his past services to them. He is not the only abstraction thus to influence his inventors.

The method is further limited by being analytic. So great a harvest has been yielded by the analytic method that it may seem unreasonable to rate this as a limitation. It remains true that the activity of the appreciative system is a synthesizing and integrating activity. How far this depends on prior analysis is a question which has still to be answered. The answer certainly varies with the subject matter and its limitations may become more apparent, as experience grows of the difficulties of solving essentially integrative problems of pattern recognition on digital computers. Problems of translation, especially where meaning depends on an extended context, provide the liveliest illustration.[1]

Another limitation is less easy to state. Until less than fifty years ago scientific faith assumed that the order which it was exploring was something to be discovered in the real world, not something to be imposed on that world by the human mind. Hypotheses might indeed be invented but they were acceptable only when, validated by the methods of science, they proved to be discoveries. The relation between the weights of the various atoms, for instance, had always been a fact. It became a discovery when observations and predictions confirmed Mendeleyev's periodic table. By contrast, the facts of human life are embarrassingly fluid. The question whether and where a revolutionary junta becomes a legitimate government or when a seceding colony or province becomes an independent state depends on whether and when the rest of the world accepts it as such. Both the categories in which experience is arranged and the rules which decide what each category shall hold are fluid and changeable. Order is created, rather than discovered, imposed rather than induced.

This distinction is less sharp today. Philosophers of science are well aware that hypotheses have to satisfy several criteria and can never be finally established, and they have more modest views about the knowledge (if any) which their theories yield of the realities behind their observations. None the less, the old antithesis is still largely accepted by scientists and non-scientists alike. Science is still regarded as a voyage of discovery and thus limited to those areas of experience where order waits to be discovered and criteria exist to validate discoveries.

Earlier and more optimistic ages believed that the behaviour of men and societies would in time yield to analysis by scientific method, no less than the behaviour of atoms and nebulae; that economics and political science would in time enlighten and guide politicians and business men, as physics and chemistry guided engineers and metallurgists.

This faith is almost dead, partly because scientific method cannot be conclusively applied to historical phenomena; but, more radically, because experience begins to question even the scientific faith that in this field order is to be discovered, rather than imposed. If the natural order is both regular and knowable there should be only one right way in which to know it, and truth should in time distinguish between rival hypotheses. It is not clear that either proposition holds in the fields studied by the psycho-social sciences. Rival views – such as those of Bentham and Marx – affect the course of the events which they are supposed to explain.

This not only limits the area open to scientific method; it calls in question also the area in which scientific faith is valid. Are we indeed to believe that, in interpreting human history, only one order is discoverable, that only one hypothesis will fit the facts? Or are we to suppose that, within some limits yet to be discovered, we can impose our own interpretation and thus affect the pattern not only of what will be but of what has been?

This antithesis is not, I think, so sharp as it appears. I have described as circular the process by which men appreciate their situations, because although experience revises their appreciations, their appreciation equally structures their experience. Thus the process cannot be described solely either as the discovery or as the creation of order or pattern. To recognize a pattern and to impose a pattern are inseparable aspects of one and the same process of knowing. Alternative, even alternating, patterns discernible within the same particulars, are a favourite playground for psychologists. Even in the physical sciences, hypotheses which for centuries seemed to be discoveries proved later to be inventions, still useful but comprehended now in a radically different conceptual form. The fate of Newton's world is the classic example.

None the less, the scope for invention, as opposed to discovery, in the ordering of our appreciated world seems to vary with the subject matter. At one extreme are the regularities which attract the attention of the physicist and the astronomer – observable regularities which (above the sub-atomic level) are not affected by being observed and which abide an indefinitely repeated series of observations and experiments, all strictly comparable. At the other extreme are the processes which engage the social scientist, the political scientist and the historian, which are learned of through and are affected by human communication; which pursue an irreversible and non-repeatable course; and in which some of the regularities observed owe something to the efforts of human constituents to impose on it mutually inconsistent 'orders', which themselves change with time; whilst others, imposed by the ordering mind of the human observer (however scientific) are refuted or confirmed, if at all, by events to which they themselves contribute.

This spectrum may be described in another way. In building its appreciation of where it is, the mind (with or without the aid of science) selects facts and abstracts general and statistical laws. But the events which it needs to understand involve facts systematically organized and require it to understand how systems hang together and what happens when they become unstable. These systematic objects of our attempted knowing can be arranged along a spectrum ranging from meteorological systems, through political systems, to what I call appreciative systems. All these, as systems, have much in common; notably, that they change constantly in the search for stability which their own activities disturb. But they differ in the ways in which regulation is mediated and still more in the ways in which their regulative standards are set. In a meteorological system, regulation is mediated by mechanical processes, such as the flow of air along pressure gradients; and the stability they seek is a dynamic equilibrium, defined by the same laws. In a political system, regulation is mediated largely by the impact of ever changing information on regulators which are constantly being reset. In an appreciative system, regulation, equally mediated by information, is the process of adjustment by which, amongst other things, political systems are themselves reset.

It is curious that, although the distinction between open and closed systems has been familiar for decades, no one has yet felt the need to coin a word, still less a series of words, to distinguish systems like the weather, which are open only to energy exchange, from the manifold systems which are open also to information and which range not merely in degree but in kind according to their capacity for making symbolic systems of communication and interpretation. The length of this spectrum must, I think, be logically indeterminable, since I cannot conceive that a system of given capacity, say my own, could understand its own level fully or could understand any higher level at all. It is an intriguing thought that among the men and women who surround me, there may be many who communicate and are regulated at levels far beyond my comprehension. It is also a thought which is strongly endorsed by my experience.

It remains to consider the *attitude* of science – the most pervasive and perhaps the most beneficent of all its legacies. It is an attitude towards facts and bodies of knowledge, towards knowing and trying to know more and towards authority as a guardian of knowledge. It is a morality which at its best is one of the noblest elements in the appreciative system of the West. It is humble, tentative and fruitful. At the same time, it is well designed to challenge any rival attitudes (not least within science itself) which are arrogant, assured of certainty and hence sources of sterility and error. It is potent even in fields far beyond the reach of scientific method, to help us reach and sometimes revise those 'hazardous commitments'[2] on which we have to rely when we can no longer distinguish between discovering what is and creating what shall be – and even what has been. It is alert and fearless to question ignorance and error, however well concealed or influentially supported. It is precious in every field and at every level of inquiry.

It operates none the less within the viewpoint imposed by the inquiry, whatever that may be. Scientific 'knowing', like all knowing, is an activity conditioned by a viewpoint. Like other knowing, it is both composite and inexhaustible. Its language is no more comprehensive than other languages, its statements no less complementary. It needs many complementary languages; for the reality which it describes is hierarchic.

The dualism of Descartes and the reductionism of Laplace are dead, though their ghosts still haunt our minds.

The systems so briefly scanned by these few chapters are hierarchically arranged. The individual regarded as a biological system is maintained by a host of sensitive regulators, alert to notice deviations from what ought to be and to use the signal to restore the deviant variable to its 'proper' state. Biologists exploring the constituents of this system to the cell and beyond find these to be a host of self-maintaining sub-systems, hierarchically ordered.

Each level depends on the proper functioning of the levels below – cellular malfunction can destroy organ and organism. But organ and organism cannot be described in purely cellular terms; for to understand them we have to invoke ideas of function which have no meaning at the levels below. Thus a single organism can only be described, even biologically, at several descriptive levels. These levels are not inconsistent with each other, nor are they simply cumulative. They are complementary.

The relation between the individual as a biological organism and the individual as a reflective, communicating person (source of so much passionate controversy) is neither more nor less strange. Regarding him as a human being, it is possible and necessary to acknowledge that he exchanges with his surround not merely matter and energy but information raised to a unique power by his ability to build and revise symbolic systems of communication and interpretation. Even if we could describe in the minutest particular the activities of the brain which mediate speech, memory, reasoning, learning, motivation, invention, persuasion and all the arts of the mind, we should still need another complementary account of them to explain or convey the smallest trace of their significance. Brain and mind cannot surely be concepts less disparate, though interdependent, in other words less complementary, than are the concepts of 'computer' and 'programme'.

Human societies and organizations are equally systems and hierarchies of systems, equally dependent on their constituents, yet equally incapable of being described solely in terms of their constituents, even though their constituents are ourselves.

There is nothing in the hierarchy thus viewed to make one level more important than another, unless it is its place in the hierarchy itself, which is, of course, the argument on which rest all 'organic' theories of society. Each level has its own significance. I have already explained the grounds which seem to me to justify the primacy which we commonly accord to the level at which we happen to be.

None the less, these views are not independent of each other. Because science is itself part of that appreciative system by which we order all our experience, its growth has affected other parts also, often to their detriment. Western culture bears many peculiarities and limitations, which reflect the largely unintended influence of science. These arise largely from carrying over into the psycho-social field ideas derived from the physical sciencies.

Thus our culture tends too readily to accept as a condition of knowing and learning that separation of observer from observed which has yielded such spectacular results in the physical sciences. This tends to obscure the fact that in the relations of men with men, which are the most important concern of men, the relation of observer and observed has little place, except in war. Men learn about each other and themselves not by observing but by communicating. They change each other and themselves by the same process. The detachment which is a condition for the physical scientist is inconsistent with the participant relation of men with men. And although both attitudes have something to contribute, the predominance of the one tends to depreciate and obscure the role of the other.

For the same reason our science-based culture tends to take as its archetype of knowledge the kind of knowledge which the physical sciences acquire. This tends to depreciate and obscure that other process, already described, by which we build our knowledge of ourselves and each other. Until the rise of modern science, no one doubted that the knowledge which men had of men was both more important and more certain than any knowledge they could have of sticks or stones or stars, these being so much more alien and so much less informative. This attitude has been so sharply reversed by the success of the physical sciences and their resulting prestige that the resulting picture of the natural order holds not only the centre of the stage but the whole stage, even though it thus leaves no room for the more interesting activities of scientists themselves.

Again, the focus of science on *discovering* order in the world – a world which includes our human selves – renders suspect that aspect of the ordering process which is contributed by men themselves and tends to weaken the confidence with which men address themselves to their most human function, the function of *imposing* order on their experience and thus helping to shape their own history.

Reluctant to comprehend and relate different kinds of order, the science-based culture of the West is equally reluctant to comprehend and relate different kinds of fact – worse, it is seldom aware that facts are of different kinds. Facts, like 'orders', may be discoveries or creations. (Still more puzzling to the scientist, they may be what Professor Seeley[3] has called 'fidefacts', self-validating acts of faith.) An English judge observed that the state of a man's mind is as much a fact as the state of his digestion. This is true; but equally truly these are different kinds of fact, classified in different ways, ascertained by different means and changed by different processes.

Suppose an explorer, planning an expedition, says to his companion – 'I wish I knew whether the natives are friendly'. What he aspires to know appears to be a matter of fact; and indeed, the attitude of the natives to strangers at that moment of time is in theory knowable, though no stranger could discover it without changing it. But what he really wants to know is whether, and if so, how he can elicit a favourable reception from them; and this depends partly on the communication which his expedition's appearance will convey to them and partly on the system of interpreting such appearances which the natives' past experience will have left on them at the time the explorer appears. The friendliness of the natives is not a fact which can be stated or predicted but one which will be created by a unique act of communication in a unique historical context in the future. Much of our communicative activities are devoted to creating and changing facts of this kind.

Over-simplifying its idea of facts, our science-based culture equally over-simplifies its idea of the function of words. It cherishes the illusion that words are coined or adapted to fit ascertained facts. But it is equally true that facts are defined by the descriptions allotted to them. These descriptions are never exhaustive. At best, they are complementary. I have already observed that the hierarchic nature of reality calls for a series of descriptions, each valid for the appropriate level. But at each level also an indefinite number of complementary descriptions are required – as many as the interests and viewpoints which define what is relevant. A psychologist, a pathologist and a prosecuting counsel give different, though complementary, accounts of a killing.

Such accounts, however factual, are always value-structured; for the significance which makes the event of sufficient interest to be noticed at all is itself the screen which selects what aspects of it are relevant and therefore meaningful. The differences between murder, manslaughter and homicide are differences of fact; but the differences are significant only because of the different values which the society concerned attaches to their different characteristics.

This association of fact and value is sometimes even more clearly marked. In a Montreal newspaper in 1958 I was surprised to find French-speaking and English-speaking Canadians distinguished as '*indigènes*' and '*colonisateurs*'. If I had been able to discuss with the writer whether he was justified in describing his French precursors, let alone himself and his contemporary French-speaking fellow citizens, as 'indigenous' Canadians, rather than as colonizers of a date rather earlier than that of their English successors, we should have found ourselves involved not in a discussion of facts, or even of the meaning of words, but of the propriety of a distinction which those words most elegantly expressed. The argument cannot be decided logically but it can be conducted rationally, unless reason be reduced to the role which science prescribes for it – a role so narrow that it cannot account even for the achievements of science. It is a matter of high importance whether the inhabitants of a country colonized, like Canada, from many places and over several centuries, regard themselves and each other as 'indigenous'. And the use of such words of inclusion or exclusion is an act of assertion and persuasion, not a statement of fact but a step in the creation of fact – a step in the process which gives form and meaning not only to the future but also to the past.

Science contrasts the imprecision of words (especially such obviously value-laden words as these) unfavourably with the precision of measurement. Yet it is precisely the imprecision of words and of the concepts which they convey which makes them such potent mediators of growth and innovation. Even in the law, supposedly a stronghold of precision, the openness of its classifying concepts enables it to grow with the changing conditions and values of its culture and to make its own contribution to that growth. Negligence in English law today is a much more refined concept than it was five centuries ago; yet its history is continuous, and among the influences which have moulded it none is more important than its own interpretations.

Science itself relies no less on such open-ended concepts. For two thousand years the atomic theory guided men's thoughts, with uncanny precision, in exploring the structure of the physical universe, before a scrap of evidence emerged to suggest that the theory was actually 'true'. Almost immediately accumulating evidence made it clear that atoms lacked the only two qualities which had ever been predicated of them; they were neither indivisible nor indestructible. Atomic theory, unabashed, welcomed the resultant clue to molecular cohesion (without which the theory had previously made little sense) and took off into the expanding universe of sub-atomic physics.

Even those less successful concepts, now discredited and abandoned, with which the history of science is littered, served in their time the useful purpose of providing a vehicle on which thought could proceed in what proved to be a useful direction. Newton's universe is strewn with substances (the ether) and forces (even the 'force' of gravity) which had as little link with literal 'reality' as any dryad or demon of animist mythology. They were none the less useful. So were the dryads and demons. If we had to choose between an 'animist' appreciative system which accounted for even the more regular events of nature in terms of mind, and a 'reductionist' one which accounted for even mental events in terms of simpler mechanical interactions, we should probably be wise to choose the animist alternative as being the more complex model[4] – though it is perhaps doubtful whether it would be more frustrating to do plane geometry on a surface we could not admit to be spherical or spherical geometry on a surface we could not admit to be plane. Happily these alternatives no longer confront us.

This catalogue of mental distortions is not a reproach to science as such; indeed, only an epistemology which relies to the full on the methods and attitudes of science can help us to chart and avoid them. It is, however, a reproach to the faintheartedness of men, scientists also but especially non-scientists, who have failed sufficiently to discern, value and defend the full scope and character of the mind's empire. Scientific thinking is no special creation, no exception to the general laws of thought. It is simply a limiting case – limited by the restricted nature of its interest and the restricted range of its subject matter.

Technology, even more than science, has had a distorting influence on the setting of Western culture. It has not only created a system too unstable to support the firm expectations needed for a human context. It has also introduced an impoverished system of values under the pretence of being value-free. This again is no reproach to technology as such but to the minds which have allowed themselves to be thus misled.

It is the function of technology to find better means to attain given ends. If the words 'better' and 'ends' were given their full significance, this would be a welcome function; but today both terms tend to carry narrow connotations which are the more dangerous for being half-hidden. It is nearly always assumed that the function of technology is to change state A to state B with the minimum use of resources. The absolute precedence thus given to effectiveness, and still more the corresponding exclusion of other criteria, is a value judgement of a most extreme and controversial kind. It could be taken for granted only if all means were otherwise indifferent. But of course they are not, least of all where technology is employed xecute policy in the human field, where every act is both a doıng and a communication to other men.

As all policy makers know from experience, policy does not consist in prescribing one goal or even one series of goals; but in regulating a system over time in such a way as to optimize the realization of many conflicting relations without wrecking the system in the process. Thus the dominance of technology has infected policy-making with three bogus simplifications, just admissible in the workshop but lethal in the council chamber. One of these is the habit of accepting goals – states to be attained once for all – rather than norms to be held through time, as the typical object of policy. The second is the further reduction of multiple objectives to a single goal, yielding a single criterion of success. The third is the acceptance of effectiveness as the sole criterion by which to choose between alternative operations which can be regarded as means to one desired end. The combined effect of these three has been to dehumanize and distort beyond measure the high human function of government – that is, regulation – at all levels.

This burden, in turn, is due in large part to the rampant misunderstanding of what economics is about – a misunderstanding which has entered so deeply into Western culture as to affect economists as well as laymen. Classical economics is concerned with markets and with the interaction of individual buyers and sellers in markets. The values of which it takes account are the market values to individuals of what they buy and sell. It takes no account of profits or losses which fall on third parties, still less of costs and benefits to the natural environment which, not having been appropriated, cannot be bought and sold, though it can be conserved, enriched and wasted. It is no reproach to economics that it should thus have limited its field; every science is entitled and bound to limit its field to what it can deal with. The need to take account of profits and losses to third parties is already begetting a tentative extension into welfare economics. There is no reason whatever why there should not be a science of conservation economics which takes account of the planet's resources and commitments, just as today's calculus takes account of the resources and commitments of a single firm and charges depreciation against current revenue. But meantime the limited concepts of market economics are generalized far beyond the area of their validity, and the enormously emotive words 'economic' and 'uneconomic' are used to bless or blast activities which even an adequately extended science of economics would blast or bless. This mischief is multiplied by the dominance which economic valuations have gained, and which they retain even when greater prosperity might be expected to reduce them. As an economist has written – 'Call a thing immoral or ugly, soul-destroying or a degradation of man, a peril to the peace of the world or to the well-being of future generations; so long as you have not shown it to be 'uneconomic' you have not really questioned its right to exist, grow and prosper.'[5] Never did a concept so limited and so factual attain a meaning so general, so normative and so saturated with unjustified connotations of value. Even the popularized version of evolution as 'survival of the fittest' has not spread so far, so illegitimately or with such cramping and misleading effect.

NOTES AND REFERENCES

1. Many communication theorists now agree, I believe, that digital computers model only part of the brain's procedures. But because digital computers are for the present the only advanced, general computing machines available and because so much (including some scientific reputations) is invested in them, they continue to exercise an influence which is bad both for human thought (always influenced by its tools) and for the future of computers. The limitations of the digital computer are lucidly and forcefully defined by H. L. Dreyfus in *Alchemy and Artificial Intelligence*, Rand Corporation, 1965. This paper is sometimes read as an attack on the future of any possible 'machines', including analog computers. I think this is mistaken; but even if it is a correct reading, the paper would stand as an analysis of the limitations of digital machines and of the combination of factors which still conceal these limitations. One of these is that a digital computer can be programmed to recognize a pattern, once this has been distinguished or created by a human mind, and also to create by random function what will then be recognized as a pattern by a human mind. Neither process imitates or replaces the activity of a human mind. Whether this will some day be simulated by some combination of analog and digital computers is irrelevant to this argument, though very important in its own right. Professor D. M. MacKay has

written extensively on this point, notably in a paper 'Digits and Analogs', to be published in the proceedings of the 1968 AGARD Bionics Symposium, which contains also the major references to his earlier works.

2. The expression is from Professor Michael Polanyi's *Personal Knowledge*, Routledge & Kegan Paul, 1958, and well expresses the attitude of the ordering mind, not only in the flux of human affairs but in every branch of science.

3. Seeley, John, *The Americanization of the Unconscious*, New York, International Scientific Press, 1967.

4. I am indebted to Gregory Bateson for this speculation.

5. Schumacher, E. F., *Des Voeux Memorial Lecture*, note 5, chapter 2.

Part III The Regulators

'If I were going to Banagher,' said the Irishman to the inquiring wayfarer, 'I wouldn't start from here.'

Can the trapped, starting from here, make their trap into a secure, viable, acceptable home? It is a question of regulation, of controlling the relations of these pullulating billions with each other and with their physical milieu, on a hugely widened scale of space and time. A problem of self-control? Of mutual control? Of control imposed from within by shared standards of appreciation, or from without by physical necessity or the authority of men? In some combination these regulative forces will impose some order on human affairs. How far and to whom it will be an acceptable order depends in some degree on the imagination of the Western world, as well as on the regulators available to it.

What we know of the nature of the trapped suggests that we are biologically ill-equipped to control systems of the size we have created or to deal with change at the rate at which we are generating it; and further, that we are culturally ill-equipped, by the way we have solved our problems in the recent past, to deal with those which threaten us now. We should not choose to start from here. But, though we cannot enlarge the first of these limitations, we can hasten the enlargement of the second.

In the next three chapters, I try first to give a sufficiently precise meaning to stability as the object of regulation, an object no less essential in times of change than in more static times. Then I review the regulators available, and the limitations inherent in them.

9 The Need for Regulation

The word 'change' is in everyone's mouth, usually in a context which implies something either welcome or inevitable. The word 'instability' is seldom heard. Yet instability, not change, is the challenge of our time; stability not 'changelessness' is its primary need. It is essential to distinguish these two ideas, change and instability; for though they overlap, they are radically distinct.

The need to 'adapt to change' is constantly expressed and accepted as a biological imperative, as if men and nations would deservedly perish, unless they changed themselves to fit whatever changes they meet in their milieu, even changes produced by themselves. Yet in fact it is the chief distinction of men, and has hitherto been their chief pride, that they have learned to neutralize the changes in their surround, so as to create a living space sufficiently stable to form a seed bed for human life. Even biologically the creatures of which our kind is one are distinguished by having stabilized their inner temperature, achieving that '*stabilité du milieu intérieur*' which, according to the famous dictum of Claude Bernard, already quoted, is the first condition of free and independent life. Men have extended this stability by the artificial climates of their dwellings and work-places. They have offset the instability of the seasons by the transport, storage and refrigeration of food. They have offset the capricious distribution of the water supply by conserving and distributing water. They have offset the capricious incidence of disease through medicine and public health. They have learned to preserve and disseminate knowledge and thus to increase the common stock of tested assumptions which give continuity to human experience. Above all, they have devised and secured obedience to law and government and thus enlarged the regularities of social life. Most of the greatest innovations of mankind have been those which in this sense increased stability and thus opened the way to further innovation in the ampler and more assured living space which they created. The most disastrous have been those which, by design or more often by accident, had the opposite effect.

Whence comes the new attitude to change, so ambivalent and so defeatist, as something to which we can only 'adapt'? It is the sour residue of that faith in 'automatic', linear, economic progress which has possessed the Western mind for two centuries and which has recurred so often in the course of this book. The earlier changes of the industrial era were either hailed as 'progress' or accepted, at least by those who did not personally suffer them, as the price of progress – as the governing classes of England dismissed the social effects of the Enclosure Acts and of the power loom. And in retrospect many of these changes seem today to have been indeed a reasonable price for real benefits. But, as the volume of change increased, as its pace quickened, as its origins became more de-personalized and its benefits more questionable, both explanations began to lose their force and a new note crept into the bland explanations, a note whose fatalism and defeatism can no longer be concealed. 'Adapt or else – !' Men, in the name no longer of progress but of survival, are exhorted to accept the role not of creators or of governors but of puppets in the world they have made.

This reasoning is as crazy as that of those communists who, for fear of stagnation, urge perpetual revolution – except that, for these communists, perpetual revolution is at least a policy to be chosen, whilst for the economic apologist it is a fate to be accepted. History, I am sure, will consign both views to the same dustbin. Western fatalism in face of change is already challenged increasingly. All kinds of relations, even the size of populations, which it was once both impious and fruitless to question, are now conceived as matters for regulation. None the less, the fatalist attitude towards change needs constant attack to hasten its dissolution; for it delays creative responses for which time is desperately short. It needs also most careful analysis; for it is indeed true that we have created an ungovernable world, in which the natural order and a man-made order are blended as never before into a system which can be neither interpreted by natural nor governed by man-made laws.

What we distinguish as change is not merely an alteration in the status quo. It is a disparity between the course of events and our expectations or our hopes and fears. We distinguish those changes which are welcome from those which are not, those which seem to be the result of human policy from those which do not; and, among the last, those which seem to be due to a failure of human policy from those which are its expression. Even this rough classification calls for a wide variety of attitudes to change. I need especially to distinguish between two pairs of antitheses. One is the conflict between rival policies. The other and wider one is the contrast between the changes inherent in *any* policy and those which betoken its failure. The first is the conflict between rival orders, each fighting for realization at the expense of the other. The second is the contrast between the changes induced by *any* ordering process and those which proclaim disorder.

The great ages of mankind were ages of change; but these were conceived as human achievements. Those who achieved them or identified with them shared a sense of mastery over time and circumstance, which implied and was rooted in a sense of stability. By contrast, in ages of disruption and decay, which were equally times of change, these changes were read as signs of lost control and sapped the confidence of men in the ability of themselves or their rulers to sustain the valued patterns of their existence, still more in their ability to make new ones. This lack of confidence implied and was rooted in a sense of instability.

The natural order remained an unchanging datum. Change was regarded as a function of the human order and was valued according to the meaning which it had for the valuing mind. And the major distinction of meaning was between control and lack of control, between stability and instability.

The great ages of mankind arose on some newly extended base of stability. Sometimes this was the fading of an external threat, as in the Athens of Pericles. Usually it included new accumulations of wealth, resources and skill. Always it was expressed in unusual unanimity as to the dimensions in which success should be measured and unusual confidence in the power to attain it. This unanimity and confidence were often confined to a minority of 'doers', an élite; but even where the done-by suffered from the changes of the new order, they could distinguish these from the changes of decay. The early irrigation of Mesopotamia may have displaced and damaged an earlier way of life, no less than did industrialism in nineteenth-century England; but its message, even to those who suffered by it, would have been different from the message of those slower, later changes which followed the breakdown of control: the abandoned sluices, the silting channels, the desert's quiet return.

Even in the greatest ages of faith, there were those who did not share the general pride of achievement. Even in the darkest days of dissolution, there were those who welcomed the collapse of the old order, because they already looked forward to a new. Athenian aristocrats protested at the lavish civic plans which produced the Parthenon, in honour of triumphant democracy, rather than of a goddess. The decisions championed by St Augustine, which were to make the Church a European dominion, were taken when the Roman Empire was in dramatic dissolution. But it is essential to distinguish the battles, often desperate and long, between one order and another – for example, between Protestant and Catholic, between Christendom and Islam – for the more basic contrast between innovative changes which proclaim a developing order and degenerative changes which reveal an order in process of disintegration.

In our age the distinction is especially hard to draw because both kinds of conflict rage concurrently. The Western ideology is attacked from without by several variants of communist and socialist faith, and from within by radical criticism, with and without a realistic alternative creed. And at the same time and more radically, both the Western way of life and its chief rivals are challenged by growing instabilities which exceed their regulative powers. And both challenges are compounded by the fact that the natural order can no longer be regarded as an unchanging datum but increasingly depends on, as well as dictating, the shape of every order which men seek to impose on their lives.

It is none the less possible in our age, as in every human dusk, to question the signs of change, in order to distinguish those which signal development from those which portend dissolution. And the second demand not acceptance but action. Acceptance would be apt only for those who recognized these changes both as irreversible and as lethal. This is a possible view. It may be true; it is shared by increasing numbers today; and it leads either to the politics of anarchy or to the policy of alienation and withdrawal. Either is understandable; both are common; but neither is the attitude of this book. For we cannot be sure; and even if we could, there are duties to be done. The appropriate attitude to our predicament, however fearful it may be, does not depend on our optimism or even on our hope. It was best expressed in the words of a member of the Connecticut Assembly in 1780, when proceedings were threatened by panic induced by a darkening of the sky so unprecedented as to suggest the arrival of a prophesied Judgement Day. He ruled – 'Either this is the end of the world or it is not. If it is not, our business should proceed. If it is, I prefer to be found doing my duty. Let lights be brought.'

Let lights be brought. Not more power; but that much rarer, subtler, more demanding fruit of the human spirit – more light.

Human life is a tissue of relationships with the physical world and with other people. The object of policy at every level is to preserve and increase the relations we value and to exclude or reduce the relations we hate. But these 'goods' cannot be simply accumulated, like packets on a supermarket's shelves. They are systematically related; some require each other; some exclude each other; nearly all compete with each other for limited resources, especially time and attention which are, of all resources, the least expansible. We may want more abundance with more leisure, more freedom with more order, more interaction with less interference, and so on; but we know that if we pursue each independently of the others, we shall attain none of them. In trying to make life 'good', we are seeking not to accumulate 'goods' but to impose on the flux of affairs a form which will yield what seems the most acceptable combination of the goods within our reach. Thus the good life to which we aspire, at every level, is a work of art and like every work of art is achieved by selecting, and therefore also by rejecting what is incompatible with the chosen form.

The orders which we thus impose on life are not and should not be permanent. What is excluded has its own claims to realization, which may have been heightened by its exclusion and fights to have them acknowledged. What is included has its own inconsistencies which become apparent as it is realized. Some of these inconsistencies are conceptual, like the inconsistency already explored between competition and the full use of resources. Some are practical, like the threats to health, affluence and well-being which those same 'goods' generate, simply by being realized, through their effect on population. In any social system at any time trends can be noted which are destined to lose or change their value as they develop, because of their emergent inconsistency with other valued relations.

On the other hand, the order we seek to impose is meaningless unless it can endure for a time. Time is one of its dimensions. Time is needed even to create it. We can seldom foretell how long it will last or foresee the changes in circumstances and aspirations that will make it some day inept or inadequate. We must be able to conceive it as lasting long enough to make it an acceptable solution to the problems which evoked it.

So, like so many seemingly factual words, stability, especially in connexion with human affairs, proves to be structured by all the kinds of value I have described (p. 98). It is structured by our interests, which determine what we shall regard as relevant; and notably by the range of time and space which we are accustomed to regard as relevant to the here and now. It is structured by our expectations, which determine what we accept as normal or abnormal variation. It is structured by our standards, which determine what changes we shall regard as unacceptable. The standards of stability thus tacitly defined are manifest in at least three kinds of instability. I shall describe as unstable any state of affairs in which the nature and rate of change makes regulation impossible and thus defeats the creation of *any* order. I shall also include as unstable that state of affairs in which any order generates its own negation so quickly that none of them can be effectively realized. I shall further include as unstable those orders which are realized only at the cost of leaving the physical, the institutional or the cultural environment unfit to support a worthy successor. None of these definitions is precise, but they include all the states which I think would be generally recognized as unstable today.

Where any such instability threatens, it becomes a prime object of policy to re-establish the conditions of stability. For, as I have already noted, the achievements which have enlarged and ennobled human life have been the creation of order, physical, institutional and conceptual.

Stability is not the enemy of change. It is the condition of any change which can hope to be welcome and enduring. The inertia of institutions and of concepts does indeed resist change sometimes usefully, sometimes mischievously. But stability, in the sense which I am giving it, is a condition of future development, as well as of conservation. It is intimately connected with rates of change. It may require that they be slowed or that they be speeded. Both are functions of regulation, which is concerned with creating and maintaining order in the dimension of time.

The breakdown of human regulation does not extinguish regulation of a simpler sort. Unstable systems go on changing, unless and until they attain a stable state; and this they hold until it is again disturbed. The system formed by men and the rest of the natural order will continue to regulate itself after a fashion, even if human regulation wholly fails at all levels above the primary group. But the resulting 'order' would exclude all those levels of human order which man-made stability makes possible. We can imagine a variety of self-regulated outcomes to our present instabilities, but they would all be highly unacceptable. A nuclear holocaust would 'stabilize' or at least check for a time many currently self-exciting trends. Pollution, unchecked, will in time curtail, in one way or another, the activity which produces it. The challenge to human policy-making is to regulate human affairs more acceptably to our human standards than their self-generated limitations would otherwise achieve. So stability takes its place, alongside and increasingly ahead of growth, as a criterion, as well as a condition of successful government. This would be acclaimed as a worthy goal by any culture which had not come to confuse the stable with the static, the static with the stagnant, and the stagnant with the putrefying. We need more stability. All our higher achievements and satisfactions are brought about and depend on stability. A cancer's goals are self-defeating, even for a cancer.

The meaning of stability is likely to remain obscured in Western cultures until they rediscover the fact that life consists in experiencing relations, rather than in seeking goals or 'ends'. The intrinsic confusion about means and ends arises from the fact that no end can ever be more than a means, if an end is equated with a goal. To get the job or marry the girl is indifferently an end, a means and a goal; it is an opportunity for a new relationship. But the object of the exercise is to do the job and live with the girl ; to sustain through time a relationship which needs no further justification, because it is or is expected to be satisfying in itself. The barren self-contradiction of life, where this truth is overlooked, seems to me to be well, though unconsciously, expressed in lines by Louis Untermeyer which have, significantly, become a favourite quotation in North America –

> From compromise and things half done
> keep me with stern and stubborn pride,
> and when at last the fight is won,
> God keep me still dissatisfied.

Whilst there is some conceivable context in which almost any utterance makes sense, this seems to me to epitomize one of the most barren and self-defeating creeds ever conceived by man. In identifying compromise with things half done, in equating doing with fighting and in making a virtue of chasing what cannot satisfy, it expresses in twenty-six words nearly everything that is wrong with Western culture. No wonder the most vocal minority among the young is dedicated to the destruction of an insane society.

As it moves towards the end of the twentieth century, the world discloses trends radically different from those which the nineteenth century expected and peculiarly hard for the heirs of the nineteenth century to control or even to recognize. Yet they are masked only by the trans-valuation of liberal values which those trends have imposed; notably, by the erosion of personal responsibility.

Since life consists in relations, we want the 'other' to which we relate to respond appropriately, consistently and untiringly to our demands, whether that 'other' be part of the physical or the social environment. As our relations and our expectations multiply, so do our demands. It should not surprise us that these demands are mutual, that mounting demands should breed mounting responsibilities, in the physical, no less than the social domain.

Even for a hunting and food-gathering tribe the environment is not simply a datum. It is affected by the tribe's activities. Commonly, only those who live by fishing can live a settled life. The hunter's food supply is more easily thinned and alerted to danger and usually imposes on him the need to wander over an area. The mutuality of his relation may be clear enough to warn him, for example, to spare female game in the breeding season. None the less, for such peoples the surrround can be taken as given to a greater extent than it can by the farmer and husbandman, who lives in a far more intimate symbiosis with his land, and must feed it, if he would have it feed him. Like the hunter, he depends on his relation with his surround; but far more than the hunter's environment, its supportive relation to him is a function of his relation towards it.

If we review the patterns of human life from the earliest we know to the present time, we find that men's relations with their surround, whether physical or human, have been growing more demanding on them in precisely the same measure in which men have increased their demands on their surround.

The industrial age was no exception; the coal measures shaped the mining communities at least as much as those communities shaped the coal fields. The post-industrial age will be even more demanding. In Chapter 4 I described how this has already led not only to a proliferation of power by doers over done-by but to a correspondingly increased demand for mutual responsibility between the done-by and the doers. This demand is not merely the ethical outgrowth of a refined culture; it expresses a condition necessary to the survival of the system at that level. If it is not met, the system will break up and reform at a simpler level, where the reduced mutual demands of men and their physical and social surround can be met. So the growth of human systems is limited by the capacity of men to respond to the demand of the 'other', whether the other term of the relationship be the physical surround or other men.

Disastrously, the industrial era managed for a time to conceal this fact, even to pretend that the trend had been reversed. For a contractual society, in which so many commitments had become voluntary and so many goods had become buyable, appeared to be one in which the individual, *given money*, could maximize his demands and minimize his obligations almost without limit. In its last phase, our age is trying to universalize this dream by making the double freedom of the rich sufficiently open to all. But this makes little sense even in the twilight of the industrial era and it will make still less in the post-industrial age. Mutual demands mount not only between men and their physical milieu but also between each and all the others; and these social demands become harder to meet as they grow less structured by custom, less governed by authority and more widely extended beyond the social groups which used both to contain them and to sustain them. They cannot be 'bought off'.

The demand of the other can be ignored for a time, like any other mis-match signal. But the more sluggish the response, the more violent the ultimate adjustment and the greater the chance that the system will have passed some point of no return.

This is the lesson, surely the oldest in human history, which technology has obscured, both by its practical innovations and by its conceptual distortions, which have penetrated our whole culture.

If we begin to poison ourselves with pollutants, we will take measures to reduce them. If we are afflicted by debilitating diseases, we will subsidise biomedical science to find a cure. If our farms become inadequate, we will develop methods and build factories to produce synthetic proteins. If we invent devices capable of destroying all life, we will find social constraints on their use. No automatic biological principle will take over our destiny, for human intervention is possible, and in emergencies it can be rapid, massive and effective. Our destiny is in our own hands.[1]

This is the creed of the technological age. First, everything can be 'fixed'. Secondly, social constraints can be fixed, no less than synthetic proteins and troublesome diseases. Thirdly, regulation can be left to massive operations, triggered by emergencies. Fourthly, any other view is defeatist. This faith is in each particular inept for today and far more inept for tomorrow. Not everything can be fixed, partly because men are finite but chiefly because nothing can be fixed without unfixing or leaving unfixed or fixing unacceptably a host of other things which may be far more important. Fixing 'social constraints' is *not* the same as fixing synthetic proteins. Those countries which behave as if it were have so far given an example which is unsuccessful in practice and abhorrent in theory to the Western world, which, however, has so far produced no working alternative. Regulation to be successful cannot be left to massive operations, triggered by emergencies, but consists in making rules which anticipate emergencies – in other words, in devising just those social constraints which defy the operational approach. The alternative is not to accept biological determinism but to recognize the limitations on human initiative which our own activities impose and thus to act effectively within its real scope. Only an age blinded by exploding technology and ruled by the vested interests of technology could accept as given the self-generated changes, however outrageous, of a system which is man-made, if not man-designed; could scurry like rabbits in obedience to its blind and capricious changes yet pride itself on not being defeatist.

NOTES AND REFERENCES

1. Miller, George A., 'Some Psychological Perspectives on the year 2000', *Daedalus*, summer 1967, p. 884. It is noteworthy that the author is not a technologist but an eminent psychologist, contributing to a scientific symposium on the year 2000. I imply no criticism of the passage as a protest against biological determinism.

10 Modes of Regulation

Obviously, a system so complex as a Western nation state cannot regulate itself simply by the spontaneous, mutual adjustment of individuals. Only a complex set of institutions, with their associated role systems and powers of direction and control could support even the present unstable order. These will surely have to play a larger part in the future regulation of these societies.

These institutions are broadly of two kinds, which, greatly simplifying, I will distinguish as general and functional. As general I include all the recognized institutions of government, central and local. As functional I include all institutions, public and private, which provide goods and services; all organizations of employed and self-employed persons, including the professions, which represent their members in their functional role; and all educational authorities, especially the universities and other places of higher education.[1]

There are those whose hope for the future lies in the growth of functional institutions, partly because they limit the growing power of the state[2] and partly because, in a warring and fragmenting world, they alone establish a universe of discourse wider than national frontiers. This second hope centres largely in the international community of science. What the Prince Consort hoped from a world market-place of goods and services, contemporary optimists hope from a world market of ideas.

These hopes, I think, are largely illusory, not merely because, as I have already suggested, science makes at present a limited and partly distorted contribution to our understanding of the more important aspects of our predicament. More generally, I would stress the importance of general, as against functional, institutions and especially the crucial importance of the state as a regulator. Such unwelcome facts tend to be buried by an unconscious conspiracy.

For a man, or an institution, regulation is simple to the extent that its criteria of success are simple. It is easiest for the revolutionary who is not concerned with regulation but with its opposite. Where the only criterion of success is disruption, the only problem is how to make most disturbance with given resources. Any fool can be revolutionary. The classic criteria of industry and organized labour were, in theory, almost equally simple, hence the resistance of both to accepting new and disparate criteria of success. I have argued elsewhere[3] that both have done so to an extent greater than they commonly admit, though less than the situation requires. National needs for productivity, foreign exchange and the continuity of essential services, human needs for full employment, health and safety have changed what people expect of industry and of trade unions and so ultimately have influenced what industrial management and even trade union management and membership expect of themselves. Thus the contribution which functional organizations can make to the regulation of society is not negligible; it is indeed great, growing and essential.

Yet even at best, it is relatively simple and unimportant, when compared with the regulative tasks of general institutions. Multiple criteria of success are inherent in the government of any political or social unit, however small. For the multiple needs and diverse standards of expectation of people living together in a place, interact with and limit each other in ways which cannot be ignored. Functional organizations can ignore the problems which they set each other; and when in doubt, they can simplify their choices by referring to their function as defining their primary responsibility. But general organizations, even the smallest, have no such built-in priorities to guide them in their multi-valued choices. They must decide not only what to do but what to want – more exactly, what to value most in the concrete situation of every decision. They must define and redefine the unacceptable, not in one dimension alone but in many.[4]

So the growing strength of functional organizations does not offset the growing weakness of general organizations. On the contrary, it makes greater demands on them and partly accounts for their weakness. And among general organizations, powerful and, I think, inescapable forces drive important decisions to the top of the hierarchy, to the central government, be it federal or unitary.

The problems which beset general organizations at this level are compounded by the fact that, usually, their members can neither escape nor be expelled from membership. Exile and outlawry are no longer available; migration is increasingly restricted. Despite the apparent increase in mobility, the actual freedom of men to choose and change the governments under which they will live is shrinking and, it seems, will continue to shrink; and change, even where it is possible, will only change one government for another with similar problems and similar demands on its members. Most modern men are sentenced to live together until death doth them part. And one form of that parting, namely capital punishment, is becoming outmoded.

Such enforced cohabitation demands a measure of agreement on those ways of recognizing and valuing ('appreciating') situations which are necessary – or are believed to be necessary – for mutual understanding and common action. If the churches played a more important part in maintaining these standards, it would be necessary to allot them a separate category. For they purport to be the teachers and guardians of an appreciative system which applies to people in a non-functional capacity; and though no longer claiming that their membership is a natural obligation more basic than citizenship, they still claim authority to criticize all other institutions including the institutions of government. The claim is no longer generally allowed but the need remains. In communist and other countries where one-party government prevails, the established party plays part of the role of the established Church. In Western democratic states the function is performed in fragmentary fashion by all the institutions which help to mould the appreciative system.

The optimism of the nineteenth century was based on faith in powers of regulation which were dependent neither on force nor on the sense of mutual responsibility but on the inherent compatibility of human interests. The moment this faith falters, several major problems arise with frightening clarity. One concerns the level of authority which is to make good the shortcomings of automatic regulations, its source of legitimacy and its relation with other authorities.

Liberalism[5] shared with Marxism the belief and the hope that the State would wither away; and, like Marxism, it must come to terms with the fact that the State is becoming increasingly dominant. The reasons are obvious and seem to me to be inescapable. The mounting responsibilities which our growing demands have bred must be met by collective, as well as individual, responses and would throw an increasing demand on the organs of collective responsibility, even if the sense of personal responsibility were more developed than it is. Equally, the increasing dependence of individuals on collective regulation, collective services and collective choices makes ever more important the level at which these essentials are provided. That level today is the nation state. Next to the human skin, this is today the most important interface between internal and external relations and I think it is bound to remain so and even to increase in importance. Despite all the criticism and all the fear which it engenders, it has grown steadily in importance for a hundred years. It has provided the model for every emergent state, even for those too weak to support all its functions.

It is true that at present almost every state is unable to meet those overwhelming demands for one or both of two opposed reasons. On the one hand, even the largest state is too small to deal effectively with the global problems of regulation which absorb its attention; hence the restless efforts to extend and unify areas of international regulation, through pacts, spheres of influence and international machinery. On the other hand, all but the smallest and most fortunate states are too large to possess the social coherence needed for collective action on the scale demanded; hence the efforts to create coherence of view and sentiment by controlling information, opinion, debate and even movement.

At the level of the individual, the same opposed tendencies appear. On the one hand, there is the demand for ever smaller political entities with which the individual can identify himself, and on the other, the alienation and withdrawal of individuals, the pathologic emphasis on individual rights and rejection of individual responsibilities and the other symptoms of the impotent society, whose permissiveness is one symptom of a 'double-bind'.[6]

The authority of the state is further challenged by the rise of powerful functional organizations. Trade unions exercise authority over their members, which is in some respects greater and sometimes much less democratically controlled than most governments exercise over their subjects. Those who control the great corporations exercise authority over national resources which is in some respects greater and more unquestioned than that of the government. Some of these rival loyalties transcend the boundaries of states. No such concentrations of semi-autonomous power have been seen in England since the feudal power of the nobles destroyed itself in the fifteenth century.

All this is welcome to those whose chief fear is still the fear of state autocracy. But to those whose main fear is the collapse of regulation – and their numbers will increase, as the threat grows more prominent – the threat lies not in the power of the state but in its impotence. Any increase in deliberate regulation must primarily fortify the power of the state. Efforts there will surely be both to devolve its power downwards, to areas of greater social coherence, and to cede its power upwards to supra-national authorities. But change in either of these directions must be limited by the fact that too often the field over which regulation is to be exercised cannot be reduced without defeating its object or increased without eroding the authority of the regulator. It takes time to legitimize authority. No new level of government is likely, in the time available, to win authority sufficient to the tasks that have to be done. The generations now living must treasure and build on what they have got, remembering how many years have gone to its creation. And their major regulative machinery is the machinery of the state.

*

The visible regulators of society consist in a great variety of devices by which those in authority ('the governors') can affect the others ('the governed'). I will summarize them as we know them in the machinery of government, where they are most conspicuous. Most of them have their counterparts in the control of other organizations.

The list tells us little about their effectiveness, for this depends equally on powers and restraints no less rigorous, though less visible, which the governed, or some of them, exercise over the governors; and also on the effect which changes in the total situation have on both. I discuss these in the next chapter.

Government in Britain, as in other developed countries, commands a huge battery of regulative powers, executive, legislative and fiscal. Greatly simplifying, I will distinguish six main kinds.

By its virtual control of legislation, government can, within wide but real limits, change the civil and the criminal law and thus alter the rules under which society lives, and therewith the boundary between the legitimate and the illegitimate. This is an educative as well as a prescriptive power, potent to influence also the body of customary ways of appreciation, as well as action.

Using legislation to prohibit kinds of activity without prior permission, government can exercise a control of private activity which, though negative in form, is positive in effect, in so far as it channels activity in desired directions. An outstanding example in Britain is the control of land use. This is a flexible type of control since, once the power is established, the policy governing the giving or withholding of permission can be varied indefinitely.

By the exercise of its executive powers, government can directly implement its policies in those areas in which it acts as an agent or through agencies controlled by it. These areas also it can and constantly does extend by legislation. To its ancient power to administer justice and maintain law and order, it has added huge executive responsibilities for education, health and welfare, for managing large sections of the economy, and for the physical development of the country, including the siting and building of new towns and airports.

Through fiscal legislation and associated financial controls, government can redistribute spending power between individuals as well as between the public and the private sector.

Apart from these formal powers to execute, prohibit and permit, government has all-pervasive influence of three main kinds.

It can influence private activity by inducements and deterrents of many kinds – by differential taxation, restriction or enlargement of credit, subsidies and allowances sometimes as specific as a contribution to the development costs of a particular project.

It has influence no less great, though less formal, as the largest buyer and largest employer in the country.[7] Important sections of industry are wholly dependent on it.

Finally, government can influence not merely the behaviour of the governed but, more radically, their appreciation of their common situation by its power of persuasion. In parallel with every change in the common situation runs a change in the way that situation is appreciated by the various participants. This change is largely mediated by public and private debate, in which government has a proper part as advocate of its own policies and exponent of its own views of the national situation and the national need.

This summary list of regulative powers is sufficiently complete to illustrate not merely one government's powers at one point of time but all the types of control exercised by any regulative body. Briefly, they are (i) to exercise and control the exercise of power; (ii) to shape the pattern of legal right; (iii) to persuade; (iv) to bargain and (v) to coerce. But this is, of course, only one side of the picture. Forces, equally powerful, both impelling and restraining, operate on the governors from the side of the governed. In exploring these it is usual to look first at political institutions, to examine how these powers are divided between organs and levels of government, the relations of legislature and executive, the independence of the judiciary and particularly the machinery by which the governed choose and dismiss their governors and control them while they are in office. Important as this is, I shall largely ignore it; for I am more concerned with other powers and restraints which the governed exercise over the governors, and which are independent of particular political institutions.

However democratic or otherwise these may be, the governors, who sit for the time being in the seats of power of any political body, are distinguished from the governed by a difference of role; yet they are linked with the governed by membership of one society and participation in whatever measure of common culture that society enjoys. Whatever are the institions of society, the governors depend on at least some of the governed for active cooperation in implementing their policies and on many more to tolerate their policies even though they do not like them. Government in any society is an exercise both in generating agreement and in containing conflict. Totalitarian governments are no less concerned than Western democratic ones to retain the support of the governed; Western governments are no less obliged than totalitarian ones to contain conflict at least until it can be resolved.

I referred earlier (p. 82) to a current sociological debate on the role of conflict and constraint in the regulation of modern societies and expressed the view that the rival theories briefly examined were not mutually exclusive. Undoubtedly a modern society depends for its adaptability partly on the capacity of its members, through abundant information and free debate, to preserve through change a sufficiently shared and realistic view of their situation, and to develop its role systems without losing the confidence on which they depend. But it is equally clear that these two adjustments will not suffice to keep a modern political society viable. Interests are too varied, appreciations too diverse, sub-cultures too divergent. Conflict and constraint are endemic and neither is necessarily resolved either by majority rule or by the rule of law. Some are negotiable, some are not. Minorities have increasing power even within the law; and the law is enforceable only within limits which minorities are quick to exploit.

I want to examine the limitations of this process of generating agreement and containing conflict; for these are the basic limitations on a society's regulative powers, and they have, I believe, been obscured both by the theories and by the experience of the liberal era.

NOTES AND REFERENCES

1. I select these from many others because they seem to me the most powerful of functional agencies outside government. The distinction is far from tidy. Government departments, central and local, are functionally organized and share some of the corresponding limitations. Universities, in so far as they provide an independent stance for critics of society, transcend their functional role.

2. They add to the constraints, as well as to the powers, of the citizens who are their members.

3. Vickers, G., *Towards a Sociology of Management.* Chapman & Hall, 1967, and New York, Basic Books, esp. chapter 5, 'Criteria of Success' and chapter 6, 'What Controls the Controllers?'

4. I have stressed in many writings the ubiquity and importance (too often, I think, ignored) of the multi-valued choice. The argument is summarized in *Value Systems and Social Process*, already quoted, chapter 6.

5. Maurice Cranston, *Freedom; a New Analysis*, Longmans Green, 1967, 3rd ed., has described the different connotations of liberalism as a political concept, in England, France, Germany and the USA. I use the word, here and later, in many senses but my usage is doubtless affected by the fact that I am English. Even in England, the political content has for long been changing and losing its meaning. At least since 1905, the doctrine of minimal state interference, central in the nineteenth century, has been giving way to an uneasy ambivalence towards state power as an architect of collective freedoms, a guarantor of individual freedoms and an inevitable threat to them. Carl Oglesby, in the essay already quoted (note p. 28) writes of the contemporary system in the USA – '... the name of the system is liberal corporatism; of its ideology, corporate liberalism'. The pejorative implications of 'liberal' and 'liberalism' in this context are apparent from the rest of his essay. In Chapter 14 I attempt a comprehensive definition of the concept of liberalism as used in this book.

6. The essence of this double-bind is commitment to principles of action, based on assumptions which have ceased to be true. I explore this dilemma more fully later, especially in Chapter 14.

7. How far this influence is or should be used to further public policy is culturally determined. Andrew Shonfield has pointed out that it is accepted and freely used in France, whilst in Britain it is still suspect in theory and hesitantly used in practice. Shonfield, A., *Modern Capitalism*, Oxford University Press, 1965.

11 The Limits of Regulation

The basic regulator of every society, simple or complex, ancient or modern, is habit (p. 62). Habit makes acceptable the distribution of power and the pattern of mutual right and obligation. Habit weaves the net of self- and mutual expectation on which social living depends. All change which involves change of habit is a potential threat to the coherence of society. Western political and social history can be viewed as a series of inventions, designed to preserve political and social coherence through change, by inculcating appropriate habits.

One of these inventions, already stressed, is the development of consciously designed role systems and the contractual allocation of roles. Another is the development of law-making power, through legislatures and rule-making authorities. The acceptance of these sources of innovation brings the support of habit even to new experience. Those accustomed to role playing are ready to recognize, adapt and develop new roles, and, equally, to trust new role-players in old roles and even in new roles. Similarly, those who are accustomed to respect the law and who accept the machinery of law-making are habituated to the acceptance even of new and unwelcome laws. Without these two habituations, no society could support the current rate of change in either role or rule.

Even in societies which are thus conditioned, there are obvious limits to the rate at which change can be supported. Those limits are set by the ability of the governed to understand and their willingness to accept the stream of innovation sufficiently to make it work. These limits can be extended by various means. The most obvious is what I will call education by common experience. An experience which is shared and commonly interpreted by a whole society may cause massive, spontaneous change in appreciation and behaviour, without weakening coherence. The new responses may still be habitual but they will be responses to a situation which is perceived as changed. The enormous changes which took place in Britain between 1914 and 1945, including the acceptance of radical changes in role and rule, were clearly due in part to the shared experience of a major depression and two world wars.

Such experiences are seldom fully shared or similarly interpreted by a whole society. The years from 1926 to 1931 were differently experienced in Lombard Street and on Tyneside. But such differences may be reconciled to some extent by mutual communication. The differences between Lombard Street and Tyneside would have remained more divisive than they were, if happenings on Tyneside had not been news in London papers and if hunger-marchers from Jarrow had not appeared in Westminster. In so far as this process tends to reconcile divergence, I will call it mutual persuasion. It does not always have this happy effect. It may polarize conflict or maintain endemic confusion. None the less, the liberal creed insists that it is less dangerous than any attempt to restrict it.

Another factor potent to unify the interpretation of shared experience is acceptance of authority. It is an attitude mistrusted by the liberal tradition. Yet the acceptance of authority is even more essential to the complex societies of our day than to traditional societies, because of the interdependence of their members in complex role structures and the specialized knowledge and experience associated with every role.

Essential though it is, authority is no sure guide, especially in times of rapid change. For the conventional wisdom most likely to prove misleading at such times is likely to be found entrenched in the seats of power. The decision taken in 1926 to restore the convertibility of sterling at its pre-war rate was carried through by those whose authority derived from their role as bankers or their eminence as economists, against the instinctive resistance of that least economically-minded of chancellors, Winston Churchill. The revision of the conventional wisdom depends on original minds outside, as well as inside, the roles and disciplines most concerned. But these innovators usually speak with authority derived from their eminence in other roles and other disciplines.

Thus shared experience, interpreted through debate and the influence of authority, is a major element in the self-regulation of any society, democratic (in any sense) or otherwise. Its limits form part of the limits of regulation.

A further set of limitations stems from the constraints inherent at any time in the distribution of executive power and legal right. The role system distributes not only power but corresponding powerlessness. The legal system limits as well as preserves rights, and imposes as well as limits duties. Apart from the difficulty inherent in changing any of these complex systems, any change is sure to be a threat to some, whilst any delay in change is sure to be a threat to others. Whatever is the constitutional machinery for making or resisting change, the controversy and its outcome is bound to strain, for some, their acceptance of executive power and legal right as these stand at the time. This places a further limit on the scope of regulation.

The distribution of executive power and legal right defines the legitimate scope of two other forms of influence-coercion and bargaining. Coercion as a regulator includes the legitimate power of the state to enforce the law and secure obedience to legitimate executive acts. It includes the small repertory of effective things which unilateral action can do, notably to restrain and, in some circumstances, to kill people, to deny them access to places and to seize, destroy or change rights to property. But even these operate also and often more effectively as communication, whilst coercion includes many communications which have no such sanction. So I find it convenient to define coercion simply as threat, and to define threat as the conditional promise to subject another to some kind of cost. I need a separate word for the complementary notion of influence exercised by the conditional promise of some kind of benefit, so I will confine bargaining to this meaning. I will justify later what may seem an unduly limited concept of bargaining and will give a wider meaning to the hard-worked word, negotiation.

Coercion and bargaining have a more limited use than mutual persuasion. Their effect is to contain rather than to resolve conflict. They also have their limits, which, when passed, have sharply different results. The counter-party who declines a bargain vetoes action and preserves the status quo. The counter-party who refuses to be coerced precipitates conflict which is sure to change the status quo, whatever its specific result.

Whatever be the constitution of a society, the process of regulation is a continuing transaction between the governors and the governed. It is a mutual transaction; persuasion, authority, bargain and threat move from the governed to the governors, no less than from governors to governed. These are the types of interaction which I explore a little further in this chapter. For between them, they determine what a society can do to resolve or contain conflict. Their limits are the limits of regulation.

In a judgement of the US Supreme Court in 1920, Oliver Wendell Holmes gave classic expression to the liberal faith in free speech as the necessary and sufficient condition for mutual persuasion, and in mutual persuasion as a means of resolving conflict.

> ... When men have realized that time has upset many fighting faiths, they may come to believe even more than they believe the foundations of their own conduct that the ultimate good desired is better reached by free trade in ideas – that the best test of truth is the power of the thought to get itself accepted in the competition of the market .... That, at any rate, is the theory of our Constitution. It is an experiment, as all life is an experiment. ... While that experiment is part of our system, I think we should be eternally vigilant against attempts to check the expression of opinions that we loathe and believe to be fraught with death.[1]

In so far as the exchange of ideas is analogous to a market operation, it is affected by the same changes which have so altered the scope and character of the market for goods and services. The relations between producers and consumers of ideas become ever more remote from the classical concept of a market; and policy intervenes increasingly, here as elsewhere, with the double purpose of preventing the exploitation of consumers by producers and of supplying needs for which 'the market' would not otherwise provide. In the mixed economy through which information and persuasion reach the individual, his choices are determined only partly by his needs or his demands. For the rest, they are the expression of 'political' choices of some kind – choices, that is, which are the expression of some collective policy, usually made by a body over which he has no control. And here, as elsewhere, two insistent pressures restrict the former field and widen the latter. One is the convenience of producers, cutting down and manipulating consumer choice to standardize the market. The other is the increasing interest of consumers in choices which can only be made collectively, be they the options available in higher education or the distribution of time on a TV network.

Here as elsewhere, in so far as our needs must be supplied by political choice, we do well to insist that it is supplied by an authority which is as responsible as may be.

In the field of ideas, as in the field of goods and services, it is no longer possible to take for granted the common stock of 'goods' which need to be collectively held. For two centuries in England it seemed that this area of necessary conformity was shrinking. Religious conformity, which had generated so much war and persecution, ceased to be a matter of public concern. Faith (though not morals) ceased to be a necessary part of the shared appreciative system. In the market of ideas, as in the market of goods and services, the 'private sector' seemed to be growing in scope and importance.

Yet this was in part illusory. Maurice Cranston[2] has pointed out that in the years when English liberalism sought and realized the minimum of government intervention, it was regulated by a code of social convention exceptionally comprehensive and widely shared. Mill feared the tyranny of public opinion no less than the tyranny of the state. But since all collective regulation requires a shared set of norms, which must be either evolved or imposed, efforts to impose them are bound to increase as spontaneous generation fails, until the limits of both are reached.

A more radical breach divides us from the assumptions

implicit in Holmes's market analogy. We have to accept that this area, which was once briefly conceived as a debating chamber, has again become a battlefield, which is likely to stage the fiercest battles of the world. Conflict, in so far as it is restrained from expression in war, rages the more fiercely between conflicting ideologies; and the contestants are united only in their hatred and contempt for the remaining heirs of the liberal tradition, whom they despise as uncommitted – ready to talk but not to fight.

So the liberal faith in freedom of utterance is challenged both in theory and in practice. It is challenged in theory by rival theories of truth; on the one hand, by the communist's conception of socialist reality; on the other by the existential claims of the individual. Mutually at daggers drawn, the exponents of these rival faiths march shoulder to shoulder in every protest demonstration. It is challenged in practice by the refusal of some of the disputants to conduct a battle as if it was a debate. It is challenged from within by the mental confusion and lack of self-confidence which its own profusion engenders. It cannot recreate the conditions necessary to its own survival without seeming to deny its own principles.

Whatever else be the issue of this dilemma, it is bound, I think, to sharpen the distinction already noted in Chapter 4 between disagreement within and attack from without, between the dissentient and the enemy, between dialogue and civil war.

Persuasion and coercion can be regarded as ends of a continuous spectrum, rather than as antitheses; but the spectrum contains at least one discontinuity. There is a difference in kind between a debate and a battle. It is a difference defined not so much by the apparent irreconcilability of the views advanced as by the way those who advance them regard their mutual relations. Between those who define each other as enemies, mutual persuasion is useless or worse. Acts of war, by whatever means fought, are also communications; but their purpose is to threaten or to deceive.

Although force and the threat of force are not the only means with which to fight a battle, they deserve separate consideration, if only because of their frequent use and of the extreme confusion about what they can do. For this purpose we must distinguish sharply between the internal use of force to contain conflict within a single political system, and its external use, to defend such a system from attack or to neutralize external threats, though its use in both fields is limited partly by the restricted nature of what it can do and partly by the uncontrollable effects of its use, both as action and as communication.

The occupation of Czechoslovakia in 1968 by the armed forces of the USSR and its allies seems, at the time I write this, to have had the immediate effect which it was designed to have. But it has also had many other effects, in Czechoslovakia and elsewhere, not least perhaps within the USSR, which may prove more important than its designed effects. And these cannot be erased merely by bringing the occupation to an end. Similarly, the destruction of Vietnamese villages and their way of life has had effects not only on Vietnamese culture but on the culture of the troops engaged and on the American people, which were not intended or envisaged by the coercing power. They may none the less be more profound and lasting than the intended effects, even where these were realized; just as the effects on Vietnamese ecology of defoliating jungles and rice paddies may long overshadow the tactical effects even where these were achieved. And even the local ecological effects may be less important than the cultural effects of these acts, as communications, in America and elsewhere.

I return in a later chapter to the role of force in external relations. I am particularly concerned here with its internal roles, one of which is especially important and has, in my view, no parallel in external affairs.

Historically, force has been used internally in political societies (by or against governments) to achieve or resist secession; to transfer or resist the transfer of political power; to intimidate governments and thus influence their policy, and by governments to suppress or deter resistance to its authority; and, as police power, to enforce the law. In a country which has not for some decades been unduly disturbed by violent episodes of the first three kinds, it is well to remember that they are neither uncommon nor far away. None of them should be confused with the fourth, with police power, in the sense which liberals give to the term.

Even police power in this limited sense deserves analysis; for its efficacy depends largely on its effect as a communication, and as a communication, its meaning varies with the circumstances in which it is used.

These are of three main kinds. Police power may be used to deter or bring to justice offenders against the person or property of individuals. When so used, it supports their civil rights, which are widely prized, and is welcome to all to whom these rights seem just. Further, it may be used to enforce the proliferating mass of regulations governing the public order, such as those which control traffic, the sale of drugs and conditions in factories. The meaning of these for the citizen varies with the moral importance which he attaches to the particular regulation, which is seldom accorded the support attaching to the traditional criminal law. Finally, police power may be used to curb offences against public order. These awaken a much more ambivalent response; for the definition of these offences draws a line defining action as criminal which, up to that line, is not only legal but an expression of deeply valued rights, notably the rights of assembly and free speech.

The difference in attitude towards the use of force in these three examples is part of the legacy of liberal values and has caused the word 'police' to become one of the most ambivalent words in the English language. Those who most rely on police power to protect life and property are most uneasy at its exercise against anyone with whom they can identify themselves, and have a horror of everything connoted by the 'police state'. So, when the protection of public order becomes a dominant issue, only a hair line divides the image of the police as guardians of 'the public' from the image of the police as the strong arm of the executive. It is a line more easily drawn in the study or the law court than in the streets.

For several centuries political history has been concerned with the struggle to make executive power responsible to law. The executive's monopoly of physical force is itself an uneasy concession. The policeman as he has been known in Britain for a hundred and fifty years is a relatively recent and very precious social invention. His role depends on a subtle combination of privilege and equality, based on his being distinguishable as a servant of 'the law', rather than of the executive; and this distinction is clear only so long as his functions are confined to bringing persons before courts to answer legal charges. His detachment is indeed useful in controlling mass disorder; since, interposed between a mob and its objective, police make it impossible for violence to begin unless it is directed first against them; and this, if it is an effective deterrent, is a most economic and impressive regulator. But if police become involved not in making arrests but in fighting, or, still more, in intimidating by the threat of fighting, their role changes in a way which is damaging to their authority as police. Men trying to intimidate a superior force by violence necessarily present an image radically different from that which police forces in Britain have cultivated successfully since the Metropolitan Police force was founded, in the teeth of much suspicion and hostility, in 1828.

It is thus understandable that the use of force to preserve 'law and order' should be suspect; but it is a symptom of a new and sinister alienation that it should have ceased to be acceptable, even in theory, in many circles where intelligent people carry on otherwise rational discussion.

Liberals tend to underestimate what force can do. Force, a century ago, denied the right of secession to the Confederate states of what in consequence remained the United States of America. Force from 1815 to 1848 contained the political discontent of England and helped to divert it into channels through which it was to be sufficiently resolved or contained for another century. Force is potent, both as act and as communication, even to those who deny its legitimacy. But it is a rough and unpredictable instrument, likely to make conflict harder to resolve, even when it succeeds in containment, and always liable to evoke escalation. It is important to distinguish, at one end of this huge spectrum of violence, that small but important sector in which the police can be clearly distinguished as agents of the law rather than of the executive and thus exercise a regulative power of a unique kind. It also throws light on what I regard as fallacious analogies in the international field, which I examine in a later chapter.

The distinction is of increasing importance in the domestic field. For in Western countries the police spend an increasing proportion of their time in dealing with mass disturbance, rather than with individual crime, and thus in preserving values which the liberal especially prizes by methods which he is especially prone to condemn.

I distinguished bargaining as influence exercised by the conditional offer of benefit. In this pure form it exists only in the conditions of that 'free' market which is so rare in actual experience, though so ubiquitous in our conceptual mythology. It is an essential feature of such a market that each party is free not to reach agreement. The process of bargaining, in this case, is one in which the would-be seller or buyer tests the willingness of the other, by improving the terms of his offer, and thus determines whether there exist any terms acceptable to both. Such bargaining plays some part in politics, whenever a would-be initiator of action offers progressive concessions to those who have power to block it or make it more difficult – but only when 'no action' is a possible outcome for both.

The rarity of this situation is masked by the market assumption, still prevalent though clearly false, that everything – and everyone – has a price. Negotiation seldom parallels the behaviour of men in a free market. In particular, what is called collective bargaining between organized industry and labour is as remote as possible from the market model which still cloaks it. When a single buyer who cannot refuse to buy meets a single seller who cannot long refuse to sell something which both agree is not a commodity, their relations have every feature which the market is supposed to abhor and prevent.

What are called negotiations in all political contexts, whether between governments and pressure groups or between industry and organized labour, are discussions in which mutual persuasion, bargaining and coercion (as here defined) are all involved. Where agreement is not reached, the alternatives are either 'no action', or, more usually, conflict, which is the attempt of each to coerce the other. Where agreement is reached, it is safe to assume that some mutual persuasion has taken place. The position of each has been subtly changed not only by the terms offered but by its experience of the other and exposure to the other's persuasion. Faith in this obscure process keeps hope alive in the hearts of experienced negotiators, however weary, when it is logically demonstrable that there is nothing left to say.

Even where agreement is not reached, it is usually safe to assume that the position has been changed, perhaps even more radically; for negotiations hold in fluid and uneasy potential the relations of persuasion, bargaining and coercion; and their failure is liable to polarize the situation, as seen by the participants, into one which admits only of conflict; to turn a debate into a battle. This may result from failure to agree, even where neither party desires such an outcome. It is virtually certain to end in this way if one of the parties, or even a small but well-placed minority in one of the parties, is determined that it should so end. And those who already conceive themselves as fighting a war do wish negotiations to fail and engage in them only as a field of manoeuvre. The techniques of negotiation, with all their sophistication, depend on the assumption that all the parties involved would rather agree than fight. This is another liberal assumption which is becoming increasingly unrealistic.

NOTES AND REFERENCES

1. Quoted in Bowen, C. D., *Yankee from Olympus*, Ernest Benn, 1949, p. 370, and New York, Little, Brown & Co.

2. Cranston, M., *Freedom; a New Analysis*, Longmans Green, 1967, 3rd ed.

Part IV The Outcome

So what? That question each reader must answer for himself. The view so far expressed is a way of interpreting the present in the light of the past. It does not suffice to foretell the future; but it may help to shape the future, if only by interpreting it better and more quickly, as it unrolls in the present.

I can do no more than describe, in the light of this interpretative scheme, some aspects of the unfolding present, as they involve me and the society to which I belong. These are fragmentary; but they are as much as I can see now, from the world in which I live, in the world into which I look out.

12 The Internal Regulators

In earlier chapters I described four main fields in which regulation was breaking down. One is the ecological field – the relations between ourselves and our physical milieu. A second is the economic field – the relation between our activities as producers and as consumers. A third is the political field, in the widest sense – the relation between ourselves as doers and as 'done-by'. A fourth is the appreciative field, the inner coherence of that system of interests, expectations and standards of judgement which orders our lives, guiding action, mediating communication and making experience meaningful.

In this chapter I look more closely at some of these instabilities as they affect our national life and at some actual or possible ways of regulating them, that are emerging or might emerge. They illustrate the techniques, the possibilities and perhaps the limits of national coherence. They draw almost wholly on British experience; but I think they have some wider relevance.

I have referred to the nation state as being the most important interface, next to the human skin, between inner and outer relations. I am concerned in this chapter with some of the inner relations by which these systems hang together.

Consider the contemporary response to economic insecurity and inequality. These conditions are not new, but the measure of what is unacceptable has been redefined by a massive shift in the appreciative system. The market is increasingly distrusted as a distributor of income and employment. The anxieties inherent in a system where position, role, status and income depend on contract are being mitigated by ever increasing efforts to secure some continuity of career for all. In Britain, the concept of full employment has come to mean, for many of those affected, a rate less than half that assumed in the Beveridge Report some twenty years before. The right to dismiss men, still more to close work-places, is more cautiously exercised, more suspiciously watched and more strongly resisted than ever before. Casual employment has ceased to be acceptable. Training and re-training are accepted as obligations of industry. Unemployment is cushioned by support with wage-related supplements and by redundancy pay. Industry is persuaded, if not constrained, to develop where labour is most plentiful. Every condition on which a 'labour market' depends, every expectation of 'adaptiveness' on the part of the employee is in practice muted, however much it is still extolled in theory. The very concept of a market in relation to employment, the concept of men's services (once called 'labour') as a market resource has ceased to be acceptable. These changes express what I believe to be a valid criticism of the contractual concept of society. But their introduction is weakening the regulative power of the market and is generating new expectations and new demands for regulation which new regulative devices must supply.

Less has been done to mitigate the rupture of expectations between the generations of a contractual society. Children today have, generally, no reason to expect that they will live their lives in the income group in which they are brought up. They may be financially far more successful than their parents, in which case they will have opportunities and responsibilities with which their early lives gave them no acquaintance. Alternatively, they may be financially far less successful, in which case they will have to learn to live with constraints which their early lives gave them no practice in accepting and no reason to expect. The resultant stresses in a meritocracy have been explored with trenchant satire by Dr Michael Young.[1]

The obvious way to cushion such disturbances is through greater equality of incomes; and this trend is already marked for other reasons. In theory our societies set much store by equality of opportunity; but this appeals only to those whose gifts and good fortune enable them to turn expectation into reality. The growing demand is for equality not of opportunity but of enjoyment. It is expressed in words by the spokesmen of the under-privileged and in deeds by the under-privileged themselves, whenever the respect for property breaks down. It is significant that the new techniques of riot control in the USA include high tolerance of looting.

The drive towards greater equality of incomes is much wider than the demand for greater equality of earnings. In the early days of the industrial revolution attention soon focused on the inadequate earnings of the lower paid; and after a century of trade-union effort and widening political franchise, there are still areas where the same concern is rightly felt. But the problem of poverty is wider than this. For fifty years at least social policy in England has increasingly accepted the need to maintain the incomes of all those for whom the market fails to provide, whether they are the lowly paid, the unemployed, the handicapped, the unlucky or the old. And this social policy has for three decades been reinforced by the felt need to maintain spending power in support of a market economy increasingly dependent on the mass market.

If the market is to continue as a distributor of goods and services in the age of automation, this process will have to be greatly extended. It is widely believed that automation will provide abundance for all but work for only a few. I believe that this will be limited by countervailing tendencies to which I will return. But in so far as the trend prevails, it will pose even more sharply the problem of distributing their share of abundance to those who have taken no part in producing it. If the market is to be used as a distributor, these would-be consumers must be given a money income.

Once again, the trend has roots in authentic social policy. The cure for poverty, it is cogently argued, is to make people less poor; not to mitigate their poverty by providing this or that facility free or at less than the market price. But the same trend is reinforced by conservative economic policy, determined to keep the benefit of the market as a distributor of goods, if not of incomes – and thus to retain for the investor and the entrepreneur, as against the State, their monopoly of accumulated wealth. 'Negative income tax' was proposed by a conservative American economist. To subsidize the needy individual rather than the public service is conservative welfare policy in Britain today.

So we can distinguish a trend to modify or supplement the market as a means of securing employment and earnings and of equalizing incomes, whilst retaining it as a means of distributing goods and services. I have no doubt that this is an important new technique of regulation. But before it could come near to meeting the demand which it expresses, it will clearly disturb two other sets of relations. One is the share of resources to be transferred to the public sector; the other the relation between jobs and pay. Both are deeply embedded in our appreciative system. Neither is sacrosanct; both can change. To the first I return later. Of the second I will note only one substantial force which tends to keep it as it is. Both relative and absolute earnings depend increasingly on that obscure process known as collective bargaining; and in this the preservation of existing differentials plays almost as large a part as the needs of the most lowly paid. The market's rewards for success remain attractive, though its penalties for failure are repudiated; and the independent datum which should force the two to come to terms remains too muted to operate.

The ecological disturbances originating in the self-exciting system have become alarming only more recently. The regulators which are possible in theory are clear enough. They are, first, to harness the power and ingenuity of the market to solving the ecological problems which it sets; secondly, to restrain it by legal prohibitions; thirdly, to use it as an instrument of public policy; and fourthly, to replace or supplement it by new organs publicly controlled. These are not alternatives. All will be needed and all combined may be insufficient.

The first, though seemingly the most obvious and least radical, has as yet been scarcely used. In many cases it would seem easy to transfer to producers and consumers, through the market, those ecological costs which can be clearly attributed to them. To take a small but clear example, soft-drink manufacturers at present find it cheaper to discard their bottles than to collect and re-use them or to devise easily destructible containers. But this is so only because they do not bear the cost of collecting and disposing of the waste they put into circulation. This cost in New York City is estimated at six times the cost of a new bottle. No law of economics decrees that consumers of soft drinks should thus be subsidized by the general public. A tax sufficient to cover the cost of disposal would not merely transfer to the consumer the true cost of the bottles, as well as the drink; it would also alter the economics of the industry and so put an end to the creation of one type of avoidable waste.

This is more important in an economic system where the private sector is so much less restricted in resources than the public sector. I live in one of the most beautiful parts of southern England. My rural district council[2] reports (March 1969) that 'partly because of modern packaging methods', the amount of refuse is increasing so fast that in less than three years all refuse tips available to the council will be exhausted.

> Because of the high cost and other problems of great complexity, it seems likely to be a number of years before the council will be able to dispose of refuse by pulverisation, incineration or some other modern method. The only practical solution . . . is to fill up the lower part of some comparatively isolated valleys.

These are the more beautiful and remote valleys of the Chiltern Hills. The citizen's only remedy will be to bedevil the choice by organized protest at each planning inquiry to ensure that the scene destroyed will not be his favourite valley but another.

The total body of producers and consumers may be indistinguishable from the total body of ratepayers and taxpayers but the institutions which provide goods and services and thus generate waste are sharply distinct from those which have to dispose of it. To shift the cost of waste disposal to the sector which generates it would, first, give that sector an incentive to abate it. Secondly, it would provide the money to dispose of it by methods no less 'modern' than those which produce it. Thirdly, it would transfer to the consumer the true cost of what he is buying. It would not 'raise the cost of living' – if that were honestly calculated. It would merely remove one device for concealing by how much it is rising. And by the same change, it would present the cost of abating it as 'economic', and therefore acceptable and 'good'. Private businesses do not report to their shareholders, as my council reports to me, that it will be 'a number of years' before they can afford to use 'modern methods'.

This weird disparity between public and private resources has got to be cured, if the ecological disturbances originating in the market are to be controlled. But so long as the user-supported sector enjoys such startling advantages over the public-supported sector, the first step is to load the user-supported sector with all its identifiable ecological costs, whichever sector does the spending. We need both to generate less waste and to dispose more efficiently of the waste we generate. We need to be free to choose whichever will be the better course; but we have little hope of doing either, until the costs of both come from the same purse and the resources which that purse controls are equally concerned in both solutions.

The control of water pollution is slightly more advanced, largely because polluted water can again be made marketable; but it is still bedevilled by the problem of the 'two purses'. In this field, unlike the field of waste generation, it is now acceptable to prohibit a producer from creating waste – as industry in England is today prohibited from discharging its more noxious products into the rivers. The originator, if he is to stay in business, must then purify his effluent himself or devise a less noxious process. But in so far as he is allowed to release his effluent, he has no incentive to reduce it and makes no contribution towards its removal or purification. This is for the water authorities. Happily, these being more or less 'user-supported' are not debarred from using 'modern methods'. The polluter and his customers are subsidized by the water consumers. There is no logic in this but at least someone has the means and the incentive to make good the ecological damage; and these authorities also have some say in the question how far the originator should pay the cost and do the thinking attached to the pollution that he originates. For they have some influence in deciding what kinds and degrees of pollution shall be disqualified from being discharged as effluent.

Not all ecological costs can be thus charged to the originator, for many of them are deferred. Makers and users of internal combustion engines cannot be charged now for the damage they do to the atmosphere, for it is not remediable by a process that can be paid for. But there are other ways to encourage the production of a less toxic power unit, from differential taxation of vehicles differently powered to the direct subsidy of research. Industrial technology is resourceful; it enjoys solving problems. All that is needed is to set the problem in a form to which industry is geared to respond.

Not all problems can be so set. Prohibition stimulates the search for an alternative only when there is an alternative to be found. But it may be none the less necessary even when its effect is simply to restrain activity, because the ecological effects are unacceptable. This will, I think, become increasingly common.[3]

For a century we have been prohibiting activities because they were deemed inhumane, dangerous or otherwise unacceptable, despite the dire warnings of interested parties that these activities were essential to industry. But in fact the productivity of the industrial era was not set back by factory acts and safety regulations. The future pattern may well be different. The productivity of the post-industrial era, as I believe, will have to be reduced increasingly and by deliberate choice to meet the demands of the ecological order.

A case in point may be the control of nitrogenous pollution from chemical fertilizers washed into rivers. This danger, so familiar today, is only so recently appreciated that it was not included among the measurements taken before the Pollution of Rivers Act 1957 was introduced. So when the expected review of that Act's working appears, no base line will be available to measure the increase of this factor. Yet today it is in the forefront of ecological problems not only because of its gravity but also because of the costs and difficulties of its control.

The economics of modern farming ignore the cost of effluent disposal, except in so far as they are borne by the farm where they originate. From the viewpoint of the national economy, this calculation is manifestly bogus but a vast superstructure has been built on it. Farming methods and machinery, the distribution of manpower between agriculture and industry and expected yields per acre are not factors which can be ignored or quickly altered. However valid are the claims of organic farming, it would take time to re-establish its techniques. Food production might thus be the first area in which developed countries find it necessary to abate productivity, rather than merely to change technology, in the interests of ecological order.

The regulators are ready to hand. Statutory standards already limit the levels of toxic substances in food and they have already operated to disqualify foodstuffs with too high a nitrogenous content. But this measures only a small part of the evil. Since the effluent from individual farms can seldom be measured like the effluent from individual factories, the simplest remedy might well be a progressive tax on fertilizers or a statutory limit on the amount to be employed per acre. The first method, shocking as it may sound, has been employed very successfully for more than sixty years to reduce the consumption of alcohol.

But taxes on beer have not abated the production or the productivity of brewers. The idea that productivity might have to be abated in the interests of ecology will seem to many to be both perverse and immoral – so value-laden has the language of economics become. So it is useful to ask why it is so commonly believed that an increase in output *per man* is so self-evidently good that nothing should be allowed to impede its increase. In so far as the idea has an economic origin, it obviously dates from the days when human labour was the limiting factor in human achievement. But if the prophets of automation are right, human labour, in developed countries, is destined soon to be the only superabundant resource. Machines will scour the oceans and even the planets for new sources of ever scarcer materials; but an increasing proportion of their human beneficiaries will be supported in idleness, having no useful contribution to make. It is a testimony to our myth-building propensity that futurists seldom question whether the supreme value of productivity will survive the only condition on which it is built. Why consume ever greater supplies of ever scarcer resources – materials, power, land – to save the only one which is embarrassingly abundant, men; especially if to do so will further imperil the ecological order which will by then be their chief concern?

The fallacy is not limited to the future of the highly productive nations. Dr Schumacher has pointed out that in India, threatened by famine, the measure of well-being is increasing yield not per man but per acre. The men are there; they are no limiting factor. They would be well released to industry, even on purely economic grounds, only if their urban productivity could buy more food than they could themselves produce from the land. But this is not so, for the cities are already pools of unemployment.

In this instance, it would seem that, not content with strangling ourselves in the mythology we have evolved from market economics, we are exporting it to lands where it makes even less sense than it does here.

There is a large repertory of devices for making market mechanisms more responsive to public policy. There might be more; and they might be more boldly used. More generally, the public and the private sectors need to be and are being far more closely associated. The policies of the private sector can be influenced both by economic and by social means. The first includes all economic inducements and deterrents which cause business criteria to work for public ends. These are forms of what I have earlier called bargaining and coercion. The second include all changes in what people expect of business and hence in what business men expect of themselves. These are part of the largely unconscious process which I have called mutual persuasion.

Equally, the policy-making of the public sector is fortified by the skills, as well as influenced by the persuasion, of the private sector. The two are closely associated. People outside government, in industry, the trade unions, the professions and academic life, are increasingly associated with the solution of public-policy problems, on economic development councils, regional development studies and so on. They even move –

though not nearly so much in Britain as in North America – between government employment, business, professional and academic life. Problems of public regulation are increasingly felt as involving everyone.

There will remain an area which must, I think, grow more important, in which public policy has to be implemented directly by massive operations paid for from public funds. This will include much of the growing activity directed to reshaping the physical and social mileu. Its planning, its research, and its execution may be almost wholly left to industry. What distinguishes it is the transfer of larger funds to the public sector and their application in accordance with political, not market choice.

Consider that most basic personal need, a home. It is still part of the national ethos to regard the market as the proper provider and distributor of houses; and sufficiently generous financing can make the facility dependent on income rather than capital. The fact remains that for a large part of our population today, finding a home depends on political, not market action; for the property market no longer supplies new homes to rent for those of less than median income (except for some agricultural tenancies) and for most of these a bought home is out of the question either for physical or for financial reasons. These rents are accessible because they are subsidized; and as the value of land rises, as it must in an ever more crowded milieu, the need for subsidy will mount, whether it be given to the tenant or to the provider. Moreover, where needs so vital as homes are not fully supplied, the priorities of rival claims can no longer acceptably be left to the market. I believe therefore that the public sector will become more rather than less important in the provision of homes. The number and types of home that it builds and the priorities on which it allots them express political, not market, choices and are responsive to political, not market, pressures – whoever does the actual building.

Apart from housing, multiple land uses are bound to fight with increasing fierceness for ever scarcer undeveloped land. Only political choice can decide between them; and the decision will increasingly have to be implemented by positive public action, rather than by the negative techniques of planning permission, which are inconsistent with the phasing needed for large scale development. This scale is rising. In what is already the third most crowded country in the world, all problems of development will tend to become associated in the twin tasks of planning the urban environment and regulating the distribution of population. There is no doubt that the urban environment will have to be planned on an ever more inclusive scale, if it is to contain the activities that it generates. There is no doubt that this can be controlled only by very large corporations, operating with very large budgets and distant time horizons – however fully the private sector may be employed in implementing its plans. For this the New Towns Commission provides encouraging precedents. It will demonstrate, I hope, that on an appropriate time scale there is no activity more certain to pay for itself than land development.

Equally, in shaping the social environment, the role of the public authority, as agent as well as planner, is bound to be dominant. Some health, welfare and even education services might be paid for to a greater extent by subsidies given to the citizen, rather than directly to the provider. But the provision must still be planned and made publicly. Public action, guided by political choice, must be the main regulator of the physical and the social milieu.

There is still uncharted room to improve its effectiveness both in planning and action. The science of public spending has been barely founded.[4] It emerged into public consciousness only a generation ago, with the Keynesian doctrine that it could and should be used to offset the fluctuations of the trade cycle and help to stabilize incomes and employment. But it is already too important in its own right to be confined to this balancing role. It is so used today only because it is at present the only form of spending directly within the government's control. Hence it bears the brunt of fluctuations from which it needs to be shielded far more than does most of the private sector.

Systems for programming and budgeting *policies* (PPBS) are making slow headway in the public sector. As they develop, it may be hoped that they will focus attention on disparate and imponderable costs and benefits which the more limited accounting systems of the past have excluded and thus valued at zero – the only value that must be wrong. There is no adequate reason why the costs and benefits of public policy should not be expressed as clearly, rated as highly and debated as keenly, as the more limited costs and benefits which engage the attention of any commercial company and its shareholders.

There are, however, many historical reasons which are none the weaker for being irrational. Rationally, our concept of economics should be wide enough to include market economics as a subordinate field of shrinking importance, even if of greater precision. Actually, welfare economics is a struggling newcomer not yet fully equipped for life, whilst conservation economics and ecological economics have not yet been born. Their empty domains are tenanted by mythological entities, escaped from the realm of market economics and not yet exorcized by a discipline appropriate to the wider field.

Rationally even today, Western man might well take far more pride in his collective, than in his individual possessions. A modern city, for all its losing fight against multiplying complexity, is a far more wonderful achievement in multivalued regulation than even the most complex of the organizations which it contains. A modern highway system, rising within the maelstrom of traffic which it is to regulate, is a far more marvellous construction than any of the vehicles that run on it. At other times and in other places, men have indeed identified themselves with the beauties and the glories of their man-made surround – even when it was created by the arrogance and paid for by the extortions of a despotic prince. But historically our country or its dominant culture has become conditioned to a different view. Public squalor does not offend, so long as private affluence can escape it. The private sector is king, and in the public sector, which is its servant, the appearance of affluence would be unseemly. The Americans even contrive not to be proud of a project so large, imaginative and successful as the Tennessee Valley Authority.

There is thus a body of powers for ecological regulation which is substantial and growing. They operate, however, within several limitations which interlock in a vicious circle.

They operate, in the first place, within the limitations imposed by the need for short-term economic balance. The dominance of full employment and the weakening of market forces have thrown on the central authority, amongst other things, a much heavier task in controlling inflation. Classic economic regulators work less reliably and no adequate substitutes have yet been found. The depreciation of money in turn affects the limits and the costs of the government's borrowing powers, building depreciation into every loan and appreciation into almost every equity.

It would seem, then, that the present means of financing the public sector are inadequate and probably inept. The very term has become almost too wide for use. For it includes the activities not only of government, central and local, but also of large public corporations, some user-supported, some public-supported, financed in a diversity of ways, and supplying services which are indistinguishable from those supplied by the private sector and are sometimes in competition with them. Yet all are affected in some degree by dependence on a government whose financing procedures are the product of a long history, irrelevant to our needs today.

Centuries of democratic struggle stripped the Executive of all resources except an annually voted budget. Later changes in the relation of the Executive to Parliament have robbed this safeguard of much of its value, whilst mounting long-term commitments make its hand-to-mouth existence ever more anomalous. No private enterprise could conduct even its microcosmic activities within the limits which history has imposed on the state. It may seem unrealistic even to discuss long-term ecological regulation, when the body responsible for it so lacks the means for even year-to-year regulation. Yet this would not be lacking if we felt the need for it and had the self-confidence to welcome innovative and reject degenerative change – if, in other words, we had faith in our ability to make our future, rather than 'adapt' to it.

Another limitation is the sheer difficulty and danger of planning on the scale of space and time which is now inescapable. The danger involved will usually be less than the alternative. Whatever this generation does or does not do, I have no doubt that the next generation will reproach it, either for shaping the physical or social milieu in a way which the next generation will criticize or for leaving to that generation a problem which will then have even fewer acceptable solutions than it has now. Courage and a sense of responsibility seem to me to favour taking the first of these risks.

A far more radical limitation, however, is imposed by the process of generating whatever may be the minimal measure of consent or concurrence. The making of public policy today is limited not by the inadequacy of its institutions and procedures, fragmentary and embryonic as these are, but by the limited and limiting expectations of its public – by the setting of the appreciative system which is common to governors and governed alike but which tends to change even more slowly in the governed than in the governors, because they are less exposed to the educative influence of policy-making. These are the processes discussed in the last chapter, whereby concurrence is generated, dissent appeased or neutralized and resistance suppressed.

NOTES AND REFERENCES

1. Young, M., *The Rise of the Meritocracy*, Thames & Hudson, 1958; Pelican, 1961.

2. Henley R.D.C. 'Report to Ratepayers', March 1969.

3. The banning of DDT in Australia, Argentina and many states of the USA may already be having this effect.

4. See Schulze, C. E., *The Politics and Economics of Public Spending*, Washington, D.C., The Brookings Institution, 1968.

13 The External Regulators

When we consider the field of international relations, we find the same growing instabilities, the same threats to the ecology of the planet; growing inequality of wealth between states and consequent economic instability; proliferation of unregulated power; unequal distribution of living space; lack of legitimized international authority. But the cultural and political forces which order a single society are much weaker and less able to impose or maintain an international order.

This is primarily for one obvious, historical reason. Men have depended on each other since men were men; but societies have not depended on each other until very recently. Throughout most of recorded time their significance for each other, in so far as it existed, has been primarily one of mutual threat. It is not surprising therefore, that force, which played so little part in regulating the more internal relations of primitive societies, should have been from the earliest times the main regulator of relations between them, and that submission to common authority and law should have emerged only weakly and transiently, except in so far as it was imposed by conquest.

War was waged in earlier times for temporary gain (booty and slaves); for permanent gain (territory and resources); for power and prestige; to eliminate real or imagined threats; as a ritual or way of life, culturally sanctioned or enjoined; and sometimes as a catharsis of collective emotions. Only the first of these has clearly weakened, whilst the second, third and fourth motives, if not the fifth and sixth, are stronger than ever. It is, therefore, no mystery that warfare should be an ancient and almost universal institution and that it should not have withered away of its own accord.

On the other hand, it is clear that war has become even more useless as a regulator and even more potent as a destabilizing force than it has ever been before. Even in the past, its function has been at best ambivalent. It has played its part in distributing the earth's inhabitants, in developing them into coherent and viable societies, in defining their frontiers and sometimes even in stabilizing their relations. On the other hand, it had generated many of the tensions which it has been invoked to resolve and it has often replaced stable systems by unstable ones, order by chaos, rich and developed cultures by impoverished ones.

However this dreary balance sheet may stand for the past, it is surely more adverse today. Until not long ago, distance reduced international contacts of all kinds, and gave an advantage to defenders, which reinforced the 'territorial imperative'. Limited productivity restricted the numbers of men who could be freed for fighting, especially at a distance from their homeland; and at the same time made the continuance of any war dependent on the willingness to fight of relatively large numbers of men. All these factors limited the range of space and time within which one state could exercise power over its neighbours by war and the threat of war. All have been weakened or negatived by the growth of technology, which has multiplied contacts between states, each ever more powerful yet ever more defenceless. Thus the modern world has inherited an institution of growing power, growing danger and diminishing usefulness, for which it has today no viable or even clearly envisaged alternative.

Even where it functioned as a regulator, war established, directly, little more than a 'pecking order'. This is, at least, an order; but it admits of no equality least of all at the top. When the early empires grew great enough to collide, only the effect of distance on relative strength prevented the stronger from destroying the weaker, as Rome destroyed Carthage. Two thousand years later war could mediate, among the stronger, crowded states of Europe, only a precarious balance of power, which has today reached its logical conclusion in the balance of terror.

It is obvious that our crowded and expanding world needs

an order more sophisticated than the pecking order of a poultry yard. It is equally obvious that war is ill-suited to establish or preserve any other kind of order and has become far more dangerous as a destabilizer of international relations than it has ever been before. Paradoxically, this gives to the fear of war some real regulative power, though of a precarious and limited kind. Between the most highly armed states their mutually destructive power deprives war of its usefulness as an instrument of national policy and establishes the balance of terror under which we live. And because of the possible escalation inherent in any conflict, the most highly armed powers have some vested interest in keeping the peace even between third parties.

This reveals the relation between two aspects of military power which are often confused. Even the grossest form of violence is a communication as well as an act; war potential is a potent communication, even though unused. But the clearness and force of the communication depends on the assurance with which other parties can predict the circumstances in which armed force will be used and its probable effect. As a regulator, military power has been far more useful as a communication than as an agency. But the current increase in its power as an agency has greatly confused its meaning as a communication. The bomb dropped at Hiroshima, potent as an act, was more potent as a communication of ability and intent. The atomic missiles accumulated later were originally supposed to be communications, rather than agencies. They were to communicate a threat which, if used, would be useless. But since their credibility as a communication depended on the reality of their role as an agent, this role had to be built up. And this was reinforced by the propensity of technology for action. Thus what was originally conceived as a deterrent became first an instrument of retaliation, and later just another weapon – but one so embarrassingly powerful that its communicative value is greatly reduced. No one can be sure whether, when or with what effect it will be used.

If the nuclear stalemate holds, and no other major change occurs in the regulators of the international political system, war seems likely to remain endemic at a level below the threshold at which it is inhibited by the stalemate. Even at this level, however, it is likely to be less decisive, though more destructive, than it has been in the past. This at least has been our recent experience. It is a long time since the political scene was littered with so many unfinished wars and unaccepted frontiers as it is now (1969). The advance of weapon technology and the international arms trade renders unstable the relative military power of states at all levels. The rivalries of great powers involve the status of even the smallest. International machinery makes it harder to accept the arbitrament of war, even when it provides no effective alternative.

Thus the containing and preventing of war becomes in itself an increasingly dominant object of policy, distinct from the settlement of the disputes which war used to settle, just as, on the domestic scene, the containment of conflict becomes an object in itself, distinct from the resolution of the underlying dispute.

This growing interest in keeping the peace bears some likeness to the similar problem of curtailing violence among individuals in a single community and invites analogies with 'police' action which are often misleading – apart from the fact that the word 'police' has such widely different connotations. I have already examined the difficulty of using police power to control mass movements without crossing the line which divides police action from civil war; and I distinguished the marginal case where police, interposed between two factions, can sometimes prevent the outbreak of fighting by making it impossible for it to begin unless it is directed first against them – though even this is equally likely to focus the hostility of both factions on the civil power or to identify the civil power with whichever faction is the weaker. It is significant, I think, that this, which is the marginal opportunity for police power in internal relations, is the only one which has so far had any real parallel in the international field.[1] I believe it will remain the only situation in which military intervention in the international field can have any real analogy with a police function.

Military force remains today, and I think is likely to remain, a potent regulator of external relations even though its police function, in any accepted sense, is so limited. It is today the sole support of the existing international order in many parts of the world. It is moreover of growing importance and changing significance, because of the power and source of modern weapons. All but the most industrially developed countries depend for their most important weapons on states outside their own borders. The assurance of these weapons is as important as a military alliance, is indeed equivalent to a military alliance. For the suppliers, on the other hand, though a military alliance would be an immensely serious commitment, the supply of arms can still be represented as a normal commercial transaction, which only strong political grounds would entitle them to interrupt. Thus armed force is potent as a regulator of international relations not only in its own right, but also because of the political links necessarily forged by the international arms trade. Even the alliances of industrial powers are fortified by the unification of their weapon systems in the interests of technology.

Finally armed intervention or the threat of intervention is potent to influence the political development of neighbour states, to sustain or change a regime, to support or check a policy, with or without actual intervention, with or without the invitation of the government concerned.

Self-defence, military alliance, supply of arms, intervention, occupation – these different forms of military influence are differently valued; some are widely detested; but none of them is likely to be displaced, unless it becomes itself too dangerous to be used or unless other forms of regulation make it unnecessary. None has any true analogy with the function of a police force and, with the exception I have mentioned, none seems likely to fill any such role.

What of international trade, of which the Prince Consort entertained so high a hope a century ago, as the future unifier of the human race? His hope was based on three liberal beliefs. It implied the belief that the main problem of national communities was to grow richer; and that international trade offered the best solution, both in the rate at which it increased real wealth and in the non-contentious way in which it distributed the product, enriching the parties, if not equally, at least sufficiently to be acceptable to both. More radically, it implied the belief that international, like national trade, was the affair of individuals. It would replace the world of warring political entities by a Great Commercial Republic of free men – or at least of free traders.

These ideas have not lost all their force. The economics of growth are studied more intensively than ever, both by underdeveloped countries hoping to 'take off' into self-supporting growth and by developed countries seeking expanding markets for their industrial and managerial expertise, no less than for their products. But the third assumption is being eroded and with it the other two. The need to balance international payments limits the international exchange of goods and services in a way which no form of borrowing can normally offset,[2] and thus limits the individual's freedom for international trade. Here as elsewhere, criteria of stability challenge criteria of growth.

It used to be thought that investment in underdeveloped countries would so greatly improve their economic competitiveness as to prove self-liquidating. Economic thinking is still haunted by this half-mystical belief that growth is ultimately self-balancing. I can see no reason in history or logic to suggest that this belief is true. Rich states get richer faster than poor states grow rich. The gulf between rich and poor widens. The poor want to buy from the rich increasingly more than they have means to pay for; and the poorer they are, the greater is the gap. Credits which enable them to buy what they cannot afford are repayable, if at all, only to the extent that they increase the productivity of the recipient at a rate greater than that of the credit-givers, which they seldom do and have seldom ever done.

The myth that foreign investment is self-liquidating had more to commend it when international trade was more complementary and less competitive than it is now. In its earliest days trade was almost wholly complementary. Men did not carry goods in open boats from Crete to Cornwall unless they could exchange them for what to them was precious and unobtainable at home. When efficient ships first took manufactured goods to undeveloped countries and returned with raw materials, it seemed that these happy days had again returned; and so in a measure they had. What value had Malaysian rubber to Malaysia, until the West wanted it and plant imported from the West could make it available? Decades of British economic hegemony were financed by British willingness, based on this faith, to lend its customers the currency to pay for their purchases. Yet most of the loans contracted even in those uniquely favourable days, went un-repaid, even unserviced or were extinguished in the end through countervailing debts generated not by mutual trade but by the unproductive and unilateral expenditure of war.

In these days foreign investment to finance international trade takes a significantly different form. The increasingly international business corporations of the West build their own plants in economically weaker countries and manufacture there both for local demand and sometimes for export. The device has much to commend it; the investment is not repayable, local activity and expertise is stimulated, the demand for foreign exchange is reduced. But the ultimate control of a growing part of the country's economic sector passes into foreign hands and raises the real, as well as the imagined, spectre of economic colonialism.

International trade grows; it confers great mutual benefits; it creates increasingly mutual interdependence. But it is not the divinely appointed mutual benefit society that it was once supposed to be. It contains latent threats, as well as promises to all the parties to it, by creating relationships which are increasingly important but increasingly unstable. It can be regulated in principle in only two ways. One is by import restriction. In foreign trade, as in any other transaction, the only control of solvency which is in the hands of the spender alone is to restrict his purchases to what he can pay for. The other is to allow the market in currencies to operate freely enough to have the same effect, by raising the price of imports and lowering the price of exports. This will reduce the total volume of international trade and alter its balance. It will also usually involve import restrictions also. For countries seriously restricted in their foreign purchases cannot afford to leave to the vagaries of their internal markets the last word on how their scarce resources of foreign exchange shall be applied. This solution will also perpetuate the present extreme and increasing disparity in the wealth of nations, including the operation of famine as a stabilizer of population in many of them.

The only alternative to this, so far as I can see, is to redistribute international spending power between nations in the same way in which the most developed nations have learned to redistribute income between their own citizens and on at least as great a scale. A beginning has been made. And in the international as in the national field, it will be reinforced by the same three oddly assorted forces as are speeding the same development in internal affairs – moral obligation; political expediency; and a lively interest in keeping up the volume of trade.

How far can we hope that the community of nations, with its newly multiplying contacts, will develop a shared appreciative system sufficient to beget some mutual confidence and to support, at least in some fields, authority and the rule of law?

The liberal belief in the power of dialogue to reconcile differences between rational men of goodwill assumed, though unconsciously, that the parties would share a common appreciative system. Up to the First World War such stability as the international political system possessed was partly due to the fact that it was primarily a function of the relation of European powers, which shared in varying degrees a common cultural heritage. 'Christendom' was indeed a far from stable system; but up to 1914 the 'Great Powers' had a common stock of concepts, even of political values, more coherent and more widely shared than those available to the comity of nations today. The League of Nations was expressly conceived as a league of 'like-minded' states and its architects had no doubt that there existed a body of principles, however imperfectly realized, acceptance of which constitutes 'like-mindedness'.

Today the appreciative system of the West is challenged

both from without and from within. Deeply different appreciative systems have developed and have been brought into closer contact through the growth of world-wide interaction and of the mass communication media, and their influence on each other has been hugely increased by the formidable techniques of the persuasion industry. That dialogue, which seemed to liberals a wholly beneficent activity, has become a new kind of warfare, uninhibited by the factors which restrain the outbreak of conventional war; potent to blur the distinctions between national and civil war and between war and peace. This ideological conflict conceals what like-mindedness there is, deprives the comity of nations of a common language and robs the liberal dream both of its practicability and of its appeal.

Yet the international community does not wholly lack a common stock of ideas or even of values. Unhappily, the most obvious are the least useful. Western science supplies an increasingly accepted view of the natural order. Western technology is widely accepted as a means to human ends. But the values implicit in both are an inadequate and in some respects a sinister base for international regulation. Some of them, like the Western nations where they were born, are associated in non-Western minds with exploitation, mass slaughter, genocide and world pollution. Others, however, have a brighter connotation. The most revolutionary of these are inherent in Western attitudes to health and education. That sickness and ignorance are not conditions to be accepted but handicaps which can and should be relieved, for poor as well as for rich, for women as well as for men – these, for most of the world, are new ideas which carry potent political implications.

In many functional fields international agencies such as the World Health Organization and the Food and Agriculture Organization have been created in the last twenty years. They help to spread knowledge, skill and ideas, to monitor threats and developments on a planetary scale, to increase mutual awareness, to unify attitudes and to mitigate inequalities of wealth. In all these respects they are important new regulators. They provide a nucleus for those much more massive operations which, I have suggested, are needed to redress the inequality of national incomes.

They are more potent than the new political regulators, international and regional. These are not negligible, for they provide both a forum and an occasion for discussing international political issues in language designed to be persuasive to third parties; and they provide occasions which would otherwise be lacking for third parties to comment, persuade and use their influence. Despite the almost unlimited capacity of mankind for double talk and double think, these debates must help to evolve, at least among the individuals concerned, some common stock of concepts and values.

The most that can be hoped from this is limited by the nature of the international community itself. Its members are numerous and more disparate than ever before. They number more than 130 states which, though equally 'sovereign', vary immensely in size and competence. More than half are creations of the last two decades; less than half are united by old cultural traditions. They are sharply divided into rich and poor, and also into overpopulated and underpopulated, two critical classifications which sometimes coincide. They are further divided by several specific clashes of material interest and by endemic feuds of historic origin, some of which are reinforced by racial tensions. These divisions are crossed and often reinforced by ideological divisions of great power, which are themselves in rapid change. So even if all the governments representing these varied entities were themselves stable and possessed any wide freedom of choice, the system they compose might be expected to experience a period of extreme instability, before even a low degree of order could emerge.

In the international, as in the national field, one regulator has gone, never perhaps to return. This is the possibility of physical dispersal. So long as the world contained underpopulated space, growing populations could expand into it by colonization or conquest. Those opportunities are coming to an end but the battle for the earth is likely to grow fiercer on that account, even if it is fought with different weapons. The battlefield today is migration. The underdeveloped and overpopulated countries, in claiming international freedom of movement, can appeal to a well-established liberal principle, one of the freedoms postulated by classical economics. They are resisted by countries of would-be immigration, whose response, however, is confused both by their lingering adherence to the principle which they are in practice resisting and by a dilemma, bred of conflict between economic and social criteria. They have come to depend, economically, on types of immigrant whom they cannot assimilate socially.

The right to deny immigration and to discriminate between immigrants is already becoming more important to countries which attract immigrants and more resented by the others. This conflict will certainly mount. The receiving countries are right in believing that their own social coherence limits both the numbers and the type of immigrant whom they can safely admit. Yet their resistance will exacerbate their relations with the immigrants whom they are already trying to assimilate and with the countries of emigration, which they will injure in two ways. They block an outlet for surplus population, whilst they encourage the outflow of precisely those highly skilled and highly educated types who are most acutely needed in their own countries.

In regulating its external relations, a state's powers are mainly negative. It may be able to defend or deter attack on its frontiers by force of arms. It can avoid international bankruptcy and economic colonial status by limiting its imports and declining to support its currency above market level. It can control immigration both generally and selectively, to avoid sociological, economic or political strain. It can limit the circulation of unwelcome ideas by censoring the communication media and banning foreign or international organizations devoted to spreading unacceptable views. Nearly all Western states, including Britain, do or have recently done all these things to some degree. Such actions have costs and they are done reluctantly but events may make any of them necessary and proper.

A state's positive powers of regulation are much more limited but not negligible. They include military pressure, military alliance, commercial and industrial support (including support with arms) and support for other states' external policy. These imply willingness to make and keep international undertakings sufficiently attested to be credible. All this is the traditional stuff of international politics.

The machinery of the United Nations and its agencies has multiplied the number of occasions on which states express views and take positions in international affairs. Any coherence which their policies and character may have is thus given much greater opportunity to breed reliable expectations. These opportunities will be increased if economic and technical agencies play a greatly increased role in reducing international inequality, as I expect them to do. The influence which a state might exercise in the community of nations is not therefore limited to its bargaining power.

It is limited, however, by the nature of the national system which national governments regulate and of the international system which they compose. These national systems are individually so unstable and so different from each other that they can be expected to combine only in the regulation of a few simple relations of manifest interest to all. The limitations of the international system are inherent in its nature.

International relations do not consist only of relations between governments. Scientific disciplines and professions create between their members a fellowship which to some extent transcends national frontiers. The great corporations are increasingly international. Individuals travel. Books and journals circulate beyond their countries of origin. The mass media spray the planet with reports in word and picture of whatever qualifies as news, wherever it originates. The cultures of protest and of withdrawal are ubiquitous. Yet the effect of all these together has not yet qualified the importance of the state or arrested the growth of its importance. On the contrary, the only forces to do so have been of the opposite kind – narrower and fiercer racial or tribal loyalties, demanding further political fragmentation in the name of self-determination. The period which has seen the creation of more new states than any similar span in human history has also seen an unparalleled number of partitions and secessions and claims for secession or devolution of power. This is no accident. Political and social organization is reasserting its importance, as against the economic, for the valid reasons traced in previous chapters.

NOTES AND REFERENCES

1. The Korean war was fought in the name of the United Nations in circumstances which are most unlikely to recur.

14 The Post-liberal Era

The trends examined in this book suggest that the new age which is dawning will earn the name of the post-liberal age.

Western democratic societies are being attacked in the name of liberal principles which their present practices do not realize – notably by demands for liberties which they do not allow and equalities which they do not provide. They are being attacked equally in the name of principles which they have regarded as inconsistent with liberal values, notably the various versions of communism and socialism.[1] They are being attacked further by revolt against large-scale hierarchic organizations, which is common to all large developed societies, and by distrust of representative institutions. More radically, the changing world situation and their changing place in it is forcing them to face questions which the liberal age could ignore, such as the difficulty of inter-cultural communication, within as well as between societies; and to abandon assumptions on which the liberal age could rely, such as the assumption that human interests are generally reconcilable by rational calculation, without the aid of any more common human bond than that age took for granted. However they come to terms with these challenges, Western democratic societies will be radically changed; indeed, they are already being changed. Part of the protest derives from these very changes.

The changes that will flow from all these impacts are unpredictable and perhaps unimaginable, but we can prepare to recognize and understand them more quickly as they emerge, by finding some common frame within which to comprehend them. I have attached the term liberal to a great variety of assumptions, attitudes and practices; but they all have in common an attitude towards individuals and their rights and capacities, which has an historical origin. The present Western dilemma is the outcome of that Enlightenment which seemed to have delivered it from its predecessor; and its sequel, if it has one, will equally be a deliverance from the shadows thrown by that illuminating event. Looking back over history, the rational mind of the eighteenth century declared the human condition to be a triple slavery and promised it a triple emancipation. Men were enslaved by economic want, by political domination and by religious superstition. Trade and technology would free them from the first, democratic institutions from the second and science from the third. Freed from tyranny by nature, men and gods, free men, it was assumed, would need no more regulation than human reason would supply.

The great emancipation has done its work and posed its own problems. In each of its three areas, freedom, having dissolved one order, has left another to be created. The new productive powers create intolerable inequalities between man and man, nation and nation, present and future. They waste resources, pollute the environment and multiply populations so as to defeat even their own productivity. The dissolution of a power structure legitimized by custom leaves authority too weak for its new and mounting tasks, makes room for other powers which in their turn need to be controlled, and calls for new authorities which need to be created. The dissolution of religious authority leaves a void which is only partly filled by new and warring ideologies.

The three goals remain. 'Chill penury', human tyranny, and false gods will always be enemies of the human state. But the way we define them and the weapons we use against them will always be products of history and usually reactions to the failures of history. The failures of history just recorded define the tasks of the post-liberal era. These must be, economically, to conserve the planet's resources and to distribute its product acceptably between man and man, nation and nation, present and future. Politically, they will be not merely to control but to organize and legitimize the huge concentrations of power which will be needed, not only in government but in all the major institutions of society. Ideologically and psychologically, the task will be to develop and spread an appreciation of the human situation and an acceptance of its inherent obligations such as will make the other two tasks possible. These are tasks to excite a liberal mind. They may be impossible but they are none the less inspiring.

But the individuals and societies on which history has laid these formidable tasks are conceived today in a manner radically different from that in which the liberal age conceived them. From my earlier attempts to summarize this view I select a few aspects which seem to me specially relevant.

All human liberties are social artifacts, created, preserved and guaranteed by special social and political orders. These orders are evolved, maintained and changed by an historical process, in which all the members of a society participate and to which all are subject.

The evolution of these orders requires of their members skills, attitudes and disciplines which are much harder to combine than they were in the days when a society could be more clearly divided into governors and governed – or, more generally, into doers and done-by. The proliferation of power involves a proliferation of responsibility and authority and requires a corresponding proliferation of mutual trust, which is hard to generate and is easily destroyed.

Every order involves for its members skills to be learned, roles to be played and rules to be obeyed, including the rules which mediate its own change. Every order is entitled and bound to determine its roles and its rules and the limits of tolerable deviance and protest. These limits vary with the demands of the situation; but whatever be their theoretical limits, the doers in any given context will tend to draw them closely, while the done-by will tend to draw them widely. Both have an interest in drawing them at the point which will best contain the conflict they are bound to generate, leaving room for change and mutual adjustment, whilst preserving the order's stability through change. Neither can be sure that both these goals are attainable. Both should assume that to combine the two will involve the fullest use of all the disparate regulators which I explored in Chapter 11 – education by shared experience, mutual persuasion and respect for authority, with bargaining and coercion to help contain the remaining conflict.

Thus both doers and done-by in the post-liberal age are likely to be concerned with the authority by which liberties are created and defined, no less than with liberty.

The individuals who now form or will be born into these societies differ from one another to an extent that we do not know and have for some time been at pains to ignore, in all the ways examined in Chapters 5 to 8. They differ genetically, culturally and by the accumulating effect of their individual experience. They differ also through the roles they play, as well as by the obvious but often underrated differences of age and sex.

The human skills, attitudes and disciplines on which these societies rely cannot exceed the learning capacities of these immensely varied individuals. How far they fall short of that potential depends on how well these skills and attitudes are taught, how strongly individuals are motivated to learn them and how adequate are the means by which people reach positions appropriate to their gifts. Thus both doers and done-by, in the post-liberal age, are likely to be concerned with the recognition and development of excellence in all the dimensions of diversity, no less than with equality. For the quality and character of life in a society depend very much on the attitudes which each member can expect of the others, not only in respect of his common humanity but in respect of his unique situation in age, sex, experience, role, gifts and excellence along all its dimensions.

The bonds of common humanity will not on that account be less important. On the contrary, these frail bonds will be most severely strained; for the ecological problems explored earlier will generate much sharper mutual demands between societies and groups which have no other common bond or which, under the stress of mutual threat, have lost sight of any other bond which could unite them. The liberal age tended to take for granted the bonds of common humanity or to underrate their importance in containing conflict, because it overrated the extent to which human interests are rationally reconcilable. In the post-liberal age, both doers and done-by will have far more reason to cultivate these bonds; for their practical importance is never so clear as when they are in danger of breaking.

Authority, diversity and humanity are less self-explanatory, as slogans, than liberty, equality and fraternity; but they are closely related to those earlier aspirations and I think they point to what are likely to be the foci of interest in the post-liberal world and the conditions of what should be its hope. I develop these themes very briefly in the rest of this chapter.

Like most words which seem to express positive ideals, equality is a negative word. It denies the legitimacy which was once claimed for some kinds of inequality, notably privileges attaching to status acquired by birth. It has worked a fruitful revolution, but it has left a world structured by far greater differences of role than the feudal world which it replaced, and therefore far more dependent both on the due exercise of power and on the due acceptance of authority. Yet its tacit implications have rendered suspect all claims to authority based on position.

The post-liberal era will depend absolutely on adequate means to make and implement political choices of extreme difficulty. Its first task must be to strengthen the machinery of government, to place at its disposal a larger share of resources, including human resources, and to support it with more confidence. All but the last have been in progress, though reluctantly, for some time. The last lags, partly because of well-founded doubt of the ability of government to handle its new tasks, but equally because the legitimacy of these tasks is not yet fully admitted.

This crisis of legitimacy applies not only to the organs of government but to all organs of authority – and with good reason. Business organizations, trade unions and universities have changed in the last fifty years even more strikingly than government itself. Each group has become more closely integrated internally and more closely associated with government, both through its own organizations and through its more prominent members, who participate increasingly in the work of public bodies. Each carries some of the functions of government, for each contributes to the regulation of society. So the antithesis between them is weakening and will continue to weaken. The cleavage which threatens the post-liberal age is the cleavage between men in their primary social context and *all* their institutions.

The relations between the government and the higher echelons of these organizations have greatly developed, offsetting to some extent the declining influence of Parliament. They are potent, not only as a new embodiment of 'checks and balances' but more positively as channels of information and mutual persuasion. They have their dangers, as well as their uses. They may polarize conflict, as British trade-union solidarity sometimes threatens to do; and on the other hand, they may produce the dangerous kind of mutually dependent relation typified by the 'military–industrial complex'. They are none the less, as I believe, welcome and essential features of the post-liberal era – if they can be sufficiently legitimized.

For an outstanding feature of the new age is that authority, claiming or being forced to assume more power, is correspondingly losing its legitimacy. This applies not only to government but to business, trade unions and universities. The employee, the trade-union member, the student is increasingly ready to reject the legitimacy of the institution's decisions and, consequently, any limitations on his right to contest them. The challenge has come most strikingly in the universities but it is a general phenomenon and clearly an important one. It can be understood as disagreement on role, though in its extreme form it rejects the authority of any role.

For the authority attached to any position stems from acceptance by the holder and by all whom his decisions affect of an agreed understanding of the role which that position carries. This applies to institutions and governing bodies, no less than to individual positions; to political and academic, no less than to industrial, organizations. Legitimacy depends on shared acceptance of role; and it is being shaken from both sides. Authority, meeting new demands, extends its concept of its role in a way not necessarily shared by those subject to it. And equally, those subject to authority may change their idea of what its role should be, in a way which authority rejects or does not even understand. The conflict in the universities exemplifies both. On the one hand, universities are drawn increasingly into the ambit of government, not only through their increasing dependence on public funds but even more through the increasing dependence of government on them, their skills and their functions. On the other hand, some of the young, in the light of their appreciation of the world they live in, reject, partly or wholly, both the traditional role of the university in relation to them and its new role as part of the Establishment.

Essentially, then, the first problem of the post-liberal world will be to create and maintain a role structure (in the widest sense) which is both apt to the changing situation and sufficiently accepted by all concerned. This structure will have to resolve or contain a great deal of conflict; for the greater the need for political choice, the larger must be the number of those who must accept decisions which are unwelcome to them, and, indeed, far worse than unwelcome. The governed, or some of them, may differ passionately from the governors (and both governed and governors may differ passionately among themselves) as to how a situation is to be seen and valued; or agreeing on this, they may differ no less passionately on what to do. In 1956, to take an extreme example, Britons (and others) differed passionately on whether the Anglo-French attack on Suez was to be seen as an issue of moral obligation or of political expediency. Exponents of the first view differed radically on whether it was a moral outrage or the discharge of a moral obligation. But this they could at least discuss, whilst they did not even share a universe of discourse with those who, holding the other view, differed equally fiercely on whether the operation was misconceived or only ill-executed. These differences were more than sufficient to shake the authority of government, even among those dissentients who acknowledged that the secret decision on such an initiative was within the proper role of the executive. But another dimension was given to the debate for those who held that the decision was not merely wrong but illegitimate; that the executive had exceeded what was or should be deemed to be its role. Crises of this kind, if not of this intensity, can arise on the exercise of authority by 'governors' of every kind; and they are bound to grow more frequent in a world in which authority is exercised more frequently, in unfamiliar issues of vital importance, at remote levels and on a widening scale of space and time.

To preserve the legitimacy of protest is as important as to preserve the legitimacy of role; for they break together, and when they break, the conditions of civil war are present. We may expect that the limits of both will be defined, in the post-liberal era, with much more explicit concern. This will be needed equally in all fields of authority; for all are expressions and guardians of the role system on which the working of any society depends.

The negative protest inherent in the gospel of equality challenged also the implication that the distribution of human gifts bore any important relation to the spectrum of wealth and poverty. Gray's country churchyard contained a distribution no less wide than Westminster Abbey. This insight also has worked a fruitful revolution; but its tacit assumptions have rendered suspect all claims to authority based on ability and has even muted the concept of differential ability itself.

Yet every sane person with any appreciation of excellence must be constantly impressed by the extent to which other people's abilities exceed his own, even – or perhaps especially – in fields in which his own expertise is great enough to found an informed judgement of others. These excellences occur in many dimensions – in practical, aesthetic and moral judgement; in ability to do, to tolerate, to accept, to resist; in sensitivity to people, to nature, to the different arts and to different kinds of situation; in time perspective and in sense of self. In each of these dimensions, there is not only diversity but degrees of excellence and shortcoming, of which the higher reaches command the admiration and confidence of all who recognize them, though they cannot themselves attain them. This recognition is especially important for those who depend on such excellence in others but can benefit from them only by trusting them.

In our interdependent age, the individual depends as never before on skills and excellences in others which he does not himself possess and could not attain, even if his role allowed. The surgeon is a familiar example but a very simple one. The business manager, the city planner, the civil servant and the politician play roles demanding no less rare skills and excellences which equally need to be recognized.

This recognition of excellence depends on two quite different processes. The more obvious but less important is the evidence of performance. The surgeon is judged not only by the judgement of his peers but also by the results of his activities, repeated often enough in a field where the comparable activities of others and the agreed dimension of success allow a standard of excellence to emerge and grow. We need not appraise the man, beyond appraising what he achieves. This is the familiar method of science, establishing relations between observed regularities. But the more demanding tasks are not sufficiently standardized to evolve such standards; and in default of them, we have to evaluate the man.

A selection board choosing a man for a new role has as yet no evidence of his performance. They build up from the evidence available, including his past achievements, a picture of the man in all the dimensions which seem relevant to the job; and this they revise from future experience of him, including experience of his performance. But unless his task is simple enough to yield conclusive standards of success, they can only be guided by comparing their developing picture of the man with their developing picture of what the job requires. And if he loses their confidence, they can only replace him and repeat the process with another. They are in the familiar difficulty of the social scientist, trying to model the relation of two historical systems, both imperfectly understood and both changing with time.

Every one of us depends, as never before, on the varied excellences of countless other people; and in all the more important cases there is no fully reliable way to determine how good these are or, still less, which alternatives are available. Hence the importance of two unsolved and barely recognized problems of today – the recognition and the development of all forms of excellence. Though inherently difficult, they are neglected partly because they are distasteful to an age still more concerned to rectify inequalities of opportunity and partly because of the odium which attaches, in an egalitarian ethos, to all exercises of personal judgement on men by men. The odium is understandable, the diffidence is natural but the task is unavoidable and should be clearly acknowledged, courageously faced and willingly, though watchfully tolerated. The judgement of men by men is the proper business of men. The appreciative world in which we live is peopled by our appreciations of each other. The facts we notice, the inferences we draw and the standards we use are the most important of our cultural artifacts. Our commitment to them is the most important and necessary, as well as the most hazardous of all our 'hazardous commitments'.[2] And the first condition for an informed and humane judgement of men is the recognition of human diversity.

Just as the early Christian Church found no occasion to develop a theory of Christian wealth, so the liberal age found no occasion to develop a theory of liberal conflict – except in the limited form of market competition. The relation of enemy was supposed to have no place in a world free from the tyranny of nature, men and gods. But the 'enemy' relation has not disappeared, and this is not solely because the great emancipation is unsuccessful or incomplete.

Earlier I defined conflict as the attempt at mutual coercion, and I stressed the importance of the line which divides a negotiation from a battle, this being the line beyond which coercion excludes all recourse to authority, persuasion or bargaining. In its extreme form, however, the object of conflict is not coercion but destruction. Where the other party is impersonal or depersonalized, even coercion is too human an approach, for only persons can be coerced.

The distinction is exemplified by the two forms of attack to which 'The System' or some of its institutions are being subjected today. One form aims at convincing those in authority of the need for change. The other aims simply at making the system unworkable. The first, however extravagant its 'unnegotiable' demands and however violent its expressions of discontent, leads back, if successful, to the conference table. The second, however undramatic its techniques, does not.

I will distinguish the second as revolutionary conflict. It is not confined to revolutions. The Second World War was given a meaning unique among European wars for many decades, when its objective was declared to be simply unconditional surrender.

The world today is full of people dedicated to revolutionary conflict; some to world revolution, some to the destruction of a political order, an economic system or a social institution. Whatever the target, the object is the destruction of an enemy, whether for the sake of an alternative clearly envisaged or for destruction for its own sake or because the attackers believe that only destruction can breed a new order. The common factor in the attitude of all is that they have severed communication with those of the opposite camp, except such communication as can serve as a weapon or a defence.

The revolutionary cannot be convicted of intellectual error, as the liberal was wont to convict him. For there may be situations in which the legacy of the past is so inept, so rigid and so threatening that it must be broken – it can never be simply discarded – whatever the cost. But the outcome of this attitude is so uncertain and its costs, whatever the outcome, are so high and are mounting so fast that all concerned have a supreme interest in avoiding it.

For Britons, this kind of conflict may be typified by the struggle of Protestant and Catholic in the sixteenth and seventeenth centuries, when an ideological division was reinforced by a political threat. It is significant that this division faded out of recognition in England, as its political significance waned, whilst it remains as virulent as ever in Northern Ireland, where it is still politically charged.[3]

Never since the seventeenth century has the world been so divided by combined ideological and political passion into groups which define each other as enemies in this extreme sense. Some of these groups are national, some are racial, some are cultural and sub-cultural. The condition for their formation is, as it has always been, a group conscious of its own identity and perceiving another as alien, deeply threatening and not invincible. The condition is becoming ubiquitous, partly because mutual threats multiply but also because the waning self-confidence of established authority no longer conceals from itself or others the vulnerability of all orders, but especially a 'liberal' order, to the power of alienated minorities in an interdependent world.

Theoretically, it would seem that the only bridge across these bottomless divides would be a sense of common humanity strong enough to transcend them. Practically, I can foresee no events so dramatic, no situations so cogent, that they would be likely to forge a sentiment strong enough to override the conflicting interests of the political societies which will inherit the shrinking world. But I am none the less sure that, whatever the outcome, the post-liberal world will be divided from today by a change at least as sharp as that which separates today from the heyday of the liberal era, already far astern. This will stem primarily from new, shared experiences. These will, I think, be experiences of increasingly dramatic disasters, foreign or domestic, international or national. It is to be hoped that they will not be irremediable. We are creatures ill equipped to respond, even individually, to what is only anticipated. Some trigger is needed to convince the busy, cushioned, comfortable West of the instabilities which are visible enough to the destitute, the impotent, the disillusioned and the desperate, even in their own countries.

There will be no lack of triggers. Instabilities, economic, political, ecological and psychological are mounting in Britain and even more in many countries, developed and undeveloped, with which our future is closely linked. The sense of emergency which these disasters will engender will be akin to that engendered by the outbreak of war; and, like war, they will cause a radical shift in the way in which ordinary people appreciate their personal situation. They will see it differently and will measure success and failure by new standards and will accept limitations which would have seemed outrageous before.

The critical question is whether the innovations enforced by such emergencies are seen as the defence of an existing order or as the creation of a new one. Viewed in the first light, they will fail and induce the sour desperation always associated with vain efforts to stem the flood of degenerative change. There is, however, the possibility that they may come to be viewed as innovative change and may induce the collective confidence of another age of greatness. The behaviour of men today towards the ecological order which supports them cannot fail, I think, to arouse disgust in any mind which realizes it. The self-exciting system cannot long command respect after it is seen as self-defeating. The facts are becoming known; only the trigger of some personal experience is needed to give it reality. From that disgust could arise the concept of a new ordering and pride in a new order.

Buckminster Fuller has reminded us that we are all cosmonauts now. We always were, but now we know what it means. Gazing out through our thin, transparent capsule of air, we roll and spin round our tiny orbit in unimaginable space; and this strange fact begins to be real to us, now that a few men, in the pellets we have learned to eject through our atmosphere, have described and photographed something of what they have seen. It is perhaps the most useful thing their journeys will ever do.

But, unlike these pioneers, constantly supported by voices from the earth, no messages reach us from the vast silences of space; only the sun's energy, pouring in to power the biochemical factory which, developing in the earth's thin surface layers, has produced, among so many other things, our singular species, and which is still our only source of support. Our age is the first to have had the chance to realize so directly and so vividly the solitude of humankind and the precarious terms of its survival. These terms are institutional and cultural, as well as physical; for we can meet the terms imposed by the physical milieu only by radical changes in the institutional and cultural systems which mediate our relations with each other.

The Western nations are the principal disturbers of the ecological peace. Their attitudes and institutions, more than any other, need to be changed to fit a world in which men can survive, not as masters of nature but as anxious servants of an ecological order wholly dependent on their wisdom and restraint, rather than on their knowledge and their daring. Yet it is the Western nations whose ethic, inherited from the liberal era, will most rebel at accepting war, pestilence and famine as regulators of the ecological order; and it is they who have inherited the greatest power to mitigate the horrors of these regulators and to preserve the possibility that later generations of men, whether in their own countries or elsewhere, may create and enjoy the possibilities of a world made safe again for human living. Ethically, their liberal heritage is neither negative nor irrelevant.

In the first chapter I described our age as heirs of a hope that had failed – the hope of a self-regulating world of persons. It was a noble dream; but it did not fail because it was too noble. It failed because it was not noble enough. It misconceived what people were and what they would need to be. It has left us with a much better understanding of a much more intractable task; but the dream itself remains to guide us. It will not be realized fully or once for all. It will evoke, in the post-liberal age, some responses which will seem the reverse of those which marked the previous era. All true courses do. It will constantly be dreamed again – unless the supply of dreamers fails – in forms which will not always be recognizable.

But it will be the same dream.

NOTES AND REFERENCES

1. The distinction between liberal, socialist and communist principles has never been so clear as the conventional wisdom supposed. The utilitarian criterion of 'the greatest happiness of the greatest number' is equally consistent with them all. Only the accident of history linked it with the British nineteenth-century belief in *laissez-faire*. A century later, Western democratic societies, with no sense of inconsistency, justify the maintenance of minimum incomes for all by the communist maxim of distribution according to need. Political regimes are distinguished not by their overt principles but by their practices and by the tacit value system which these practices imply.

2. The phrase is Professor Michael Polanyi's; he develops his concept of commitment and its inherent hazard in *Personal Knowledge*, Routledge & Kegan Paul, 1958.

3. It is startling, at first sight, to find the courtly and cultured

Edmund Spenser using (for example, in the fifth Eclogue of *The Shepherd's Calendar*) stereotypes as crude as those which express and inflame anti-Catholic feeling in Northern Ireland four hundred years later. Surprise wanes when it is remembered that, ten years after publishing that book, he was enriched by Queen Elizabeth I with the estate of an Irish nobleman attained of treason; and that a decade later he would fly from that estate before the fury of the next Catholic rebellion, one of his young children perishing in the flames of his burning house. These bitter passions have no place in liberal theory but they have not been extinguished by the liberal era.

Appendix

The Oddities of Historical Systems

In this book I have used the words 'system' and 'systematic' in a great variety of contexts. One feature which all these have in common is an attitude on the part of the inquirer. We seek explanations in terms of systematic relations, when we are concerned to understand some perceived regularity or irregularity, extended in time, which simpler explanations in terms of linear cause and effect do not explain to our satisfaction. If I learn that a snake's internal temperature varies with the temperature of the surrounding air, I am content to regard the one as a direct effect of the other. But when I learn that my own blood retains a constant temperature to a fraction of a degree, despite wide variations in the temperature around, I suspect that some regulative mechanism must be intervening to offset these variations, by establishing a systematic relation between them and their correctives. I assume that this mechanism will not violate any of the causal sequences with which I am familiar, but will combine them in some mutually responsive way, which must be the subject of my inquiry.

Similarly, if I want to intervene in some situation, so as to secure an enduring and predictable change in it, I shall usually be unwise to regard this as merely a problem of changing state A to state B. I must at least understand the conditions which maintain state A through time and predict those which will suffice to maintain state B. And I cannot even guess the real costs of my action, unless I can also form some rough idea of the effect which it will have on other states which concern me for good or ill.

Although there is nothing novel or controversial in these propositions, they are overshadowed in Western culture by the ideology of an earlier phase of science and technology. The novel abundance of energy, coupled with the understanding of a greater range of physical laws, gave men intoxicating power as *operators* and made operation, rather than regulation, the paradigm of human activity. The need to transcend this limitation is one of the themes of this book. It is also one of the lessons of contemporary history. Medicine, for example, both therapeutic and preventive, is being constantly invited to view the control of disease as a regulative, rather than an operative problem; and so, still more, are the agricultural scientists.

The inquirer may be moved simply by disinterested curiosity, as when Copernicus brooded on the motions of the planets or earlier physicists on the coherence of a pebble; or when a philosopher wondered whether he could step twice into the same river. Alternatively, the inquirer may seek understanding with a view to preserving or restoring some regularity that he values, as when a doctor seeks to diagnose a fever or an economist plans to check a depression or curb a boom in business activity or a politician feels the need to integrate an alienated minority into an otherwise self-regulating society.

Similar but much simpler problems beset the technologist, concerned to devise an artificial system. A candle manufacturer must so select and combine the properties of wax and wick that the heat of the flame (an otherwise unwelcome by-product of the light which is its *raison d'être*) will melt the wax at its base at a rate sufficient to keep itself burning, without melting the candle or allowing it to gutter. Steam engines have been fitted for nearly two centuries with governors which automatically restrict the steam inlet, when the shaft rotates at more than a given speed. The most familiar contemporary examples are the thermostat and the automatic pilot.

These man-made systems are the easiest to analyse, because they are designed for a purpose and contain no more elements than are needed for that purpose. Their purpose is to ensure that some state continues unchanged or changes in some predetermined way and their essential elements are means to compare the actual state of affairs with this standard and to reduce any deviation that may appear between them. Thus they need (1) some means to observe the actual (a compass; a thermostat) and to compare it with the standard (the course; the thermostat setting); (2) some means to influence the actual (a rudder; a boiler); and (3) some means by which the comparison can be used to initiate appropriate action. Where the device has more than one possibility of action, it will need a selector to choose between them.

Every element in this regulative cycle can be greatly elaborated. The actual may not be observable; it may have to be estimated or its future state predicted. The standard may be fed in from outside the system, like a ship's course; or built in, as in the control of a ship's stabilizers; or found by the device itself, by rules which are themselves built in, as a homing missile 'latches on' to its target. The signal generated by the comparison may release any kind of action, drawing its energy from another source, as an automatic pilot, using no more energy than is needed to send a signal, releases and controls the power needed to turn the rudder of a great ship. The repertory of possible responses may be of any complexity, so long as the selector is equal to its task. The rules by which it chooses may be stored, fed in or even learned by experience. However simple or complex the process, it can be analysed into these elements.

The same analysis holds for business organizations. The flow of materials through a manufacturing plant is ultimately controlled by the outflow of its finished products, a rate which market changes may unexpectedly cut or challenge to expand. Even to maintain a given rate requires delicate coordination in the supply of raw materials, parts to the assembly lines, transport to the loading bays; and equally, in the flow of money and the recruitment and training of staff. To maintain this tissue of relations; to cushion it against accidents and short-term fluctuations in demand; and to make it smoothly self-adjusting to changes in the volume and type of production required – these are the skills of industrial management.

These socio-technological systems may also involve the management of natural resources. I have described (p. 36) how the river Thames, once a natural system, is becoming increasingly absorbed into the man-managed cycle of water utilization. The problem in form is still the same. To establish control, the first step is to set up some authority which can forecast the standards implicit in rising, aggregate demands for water; to establish the actual and potential resources available; to determine the repertory of possible actions which can bring actual and standard into line; to choose which to use and to set them to work.

Thus the problem set to the Water Resources Board is formally the same as that set to any engineer required to design a self-regulating system of a simpler kind; but two practical differences are conspicuous. The standard of what 'ought to be' is not a datum but an historical growth in English social expectations. No one a century ago expected or wanted to use domestic water at the rate of thirty gallons per head per day; and it may be that a century hence no one will be able to do so. They may even look back in horror on the wastefulness of an age which used drinking water to flush away its sewage. Even if the present standard can be maintained, it may cease to seem desirable, when the cost of achieving it is expressed in terms of what it would entail and prohibit. Its future, as well as its past, is a function of history.

Furthermore, the actual, present, past and future, is equally historical. The available water resources of England have been affected both by the physical history of the area and still more by human activity (town building and land drainage, for example) and their future will be no less affected by historical changes.

Human social systems are historical in two senses. Both their standards and their facts are products of history; and each is the product of a different history. The history of events and the history of ideas unroll side by side and in the closest relationship; yet each has its own logic, its own dynamic and its own time scale. Neither can be reduced to the other.

Non-human systems are affected only by the history of events; but this includes, sometimes, the history of their own activities. The natural Thames, for example, was no more than the way in which water from a given catchment area found its way to the sea. Its course was wholly determined by the shape and character of this area. This shape itself is the product of history. Until the melting ice allowed ground levels to the north of the river to rise, what is now the upper Thames made, it is believed, no contact with what is now the lower Thames but found its way to the sea north of the Chilterns. Seen in an historical perspective of this scale, the Thames as we know it is itself an historical event.

But it is also an historical process in another sense. It is an agent, as well as a product. Its waters carved out its bed; and its bed contained its waters. This mutual relation is still at work; the river's own flow is still active to scour and to silt, to erode and to build up; and the results of this architecture affect the course of the stream and the subsequent flow and effect of the waters.

These mutual relations need to be distinguished from those which link the river system with the independent variables forming its surround. For they are much more difficult for an inquirer to understand or even identify, let alone predict. Yet in distinguishing a system from its environment, an inquirer can seldom avoid including in the system all those variables which affect each other in ways relevant to his inquiry.

Systems which do not include human agents are unaffected *in their working* by the history of ideas. They set themselves no standards; they develop no purposes. None the less, we as human agents cannot explore them without shaping them, by our selections and our abstractions, to the measure of our interests and our limitations. For example, what we regard as historical is determined partly by our own nature, notably our own life span, and partly by the context of the inquiry. For some purposes we can ignore changes perceptible only over centuries or even decades; for other purposes, such changes may be dominant. The systems we carve out for study are mental artifacts – not arbitrary artifacts, but artifacts none the less. If, in trying to understand some systematic relation, we overlook one of the major interacting variables, we shall learn nothing from our inquiry, except, perhaps, our mistake. None the less, the variables we select are chosen from their relevance to our interests and to the time span of our concern; and we must often choose between the simplification which makes the problem manageable but gravely unrealistic and the more complex representation which makes it realistic but gravely unmanageable. I have already commented on the danger inherent in the present age of digital computers, which sets so high a premium on posing problems in terms which these essentially moronic instruments can handle.

Even the basic determinants which evoke our inquiry are the products of our appreciative development; for they are what I have called perceived regularities and irregularities. What we perceive as – more exactly, what interest us as – regularities are limited by our capacities and developed by our interests, our expectations and our standards, those structural bases of our understanding. Until a few decades ago, the oscillations of the trade cycle were regarded as a necessary, effective and acceptable mechanism for regulating an expanding economy.

It is still unfashionable and barely respectable to insist that men have purposes, whilst rivers have not, still more to insist that their purposes make a difference. Yet it is, I think, inescapable that human purposes do made a difference; that human affairs display the interaction of two processes, however 'determinate', rather than the course of a single one. In fact, as I have emphasized several times (especially p. 128) I believe that explanations of human behaviour can only be superficial, so long as they are expressed in terms of purposes, that is, of goal seeking. The more radical peculiarity of the human mind is the generation of multiple and often conflicting standards for appreciating and regulating ongoing relationships, an essentially aesthetic activity. These standards are not given; they are the fruits of the evolution of what I have called our appreciative systems, individual as well as social. It should really be unnecessary, I think, to insist that this process, in its essence what T. H. Huxley called 'the evolution of society', is 'a process of an essentially different character' not only from that which brings about the evolution of species . . . but even more, from that which brings about the course of a river.

The human predicament, I have suggested, is produced by the interaction of these two streams of development. (It may be that the development of human institutions is itself a process sufficiently autonomous to be distinguished in its own right.) Science inclines us to attach primary importance to the course of events; what happens, not what we think is happening, is real. A feeling for the human situation may focus attention on the second. Whatever is happening, our interventions and even our responses depend on interpretations which are our own creations. A sophisticated, modern view will try to hold the balance even; but it will resist the unhistorical view inherent in classical science and rampant today in scientific and pseudo-scientific thinking, knowing that history is the seed-bed of meaning.

This sense of history, which is the awareness of time as a dimension, will also alert us to distinguish the dual role played by the standards by which we regulate our affairs in the interest both of optimizing the manifold relations which they define and of preserving the stability of the system. Stability becomes an overriding criterion of success only at desperate moments (of which the present may be one); but it remains always a condition of success. It is a condition invisible in the episodic world of the operator, seeking his successive goals, but basic to the ongoing world of the regulator, the governor, whose aims are relations extended in time.

The conditions of our day are threatening, first, because the multiple interlocking systems of which we form part have become too complex to be understood; and, secondly, because our fears and aspirations have generated standards so exacting and so conflicting as to pose insoluble problems of multi-valued choice. But, in my view, a greater threat than either of these is latent in the self-generated rate of change both in the course of events and in the categories and standards of our appreciation. Stability is a relative term; it should be no more than a condition of success. But it is a condition fundamental to all our other searches, for it is the condition on which alone our further search for our humanity can go on.

Bibliography

(This lists only books mentioned in the text.)

BOWEN, C. D., *Yankee from Olympus*, Ernest Benn, 1949.
BUCHANAN, C. D., *Traffic in Towns*, HMSO. Also in Penguin.
CARSON, R., *The Silent Spring*, Hamish Hamilton, 1963.
COMMONER, BARRY, *Science and Survival*, Gollancz, 1966.
CRANSTON, M., *Freedom; a New Analysis*, 3rd ed., Longmans Green, 1967.
DAHRENDORF, R., *Essays in the Theory of Society*, Routledge & Kegan Paul, 1968.
DREYFUS, H. L., *Alchemy and Artificial Intelligence*, California, The Rand Corporation, 1965.
EHRLICH, PAUL B., *The Population Bomb*, New York, Ballantine Books, 1968.
EMMET, D., *Rules, Roles and Relations*, Macmillan, 1966.
EWALD, W. R. Jr (ed.), *Environment and Change*, Indiana University Press, 1968.
FAIRLIE, H., *The Life of Politics*, New York, Basic Books, 1968.
GALBRAITH, J. G., *The Affluent Society*, 2nd ed., revised, Hamish Hamilton, 1969. Also in Pelican.
GALBRAITH, J. G., *The New Industrial State*, Hamish Hamilton, 1967. Also in Pelican.
GLUCKMAN, M., *The Judicial Process among the Barotse of Northern Rhodesia*, Manchester, The University Press, 1955.
LORENZ, K., *On Aggression*, Methuen, 1966.
MACKAY, D. M., *Information, Mechanism and Meaning*, Cambridge, Massachusetts, The MIT Press, 1969.
MAYHEW, C., *Party Games*, Hutchinson, 1969.
MILLER, G. A., in *Daedalus*, Summer 1967.
MOUNTFORD, C. P., *Australian Aboriginal Portraits*, Cambridge University Press (Melbourne), 1967.
POLANYI, M., *Personal Knowledge*, Routledge & Kegan Paul, 1958.

SCHULZE, C. E., *The Politics and Economics of Public Spending*, Washington, D. C., The Brookings Institution, 1968.

SCHUMACHER, E. F., *Des Voeux Memorial Lecture*, National Society for Clean Air, 1967.

SEELEY, J. S., *The Americanization of the Unconscious*, New York, International Scientific Press, 1967.

SHONFIELD, A., *Modern Capitalism*, Oxford University Press, 1965.

TOULMIN, S. and GOODFIELD, J., *The Architecture of Matter*, Hutchinson, 1952; Pelican, 1965.

VICKERS, G., *The Art of Judgement*, Chapman & Hall and New York, Basic Books, 1965; Methuen, 1968.

VICKERS, G., *Towards a Sociology of Management*, Chapman & Hall and New York, Basic Books, 1967.

VICKERS, G., *Value Systems and Social Process*, Tavistock Publications and New York, Basic Books, 1968; Pelican, 1970.

YOUNG, M., *The Rise of the Meritocracy*, Thames & Hudson 1958; Pelican, 1961.

Index